Renal DIET
COOKBOOK
for beginners

Low **Potassium,**
Phosphorus, and **Sodium**
Recipes to Improve **Renal Function**
and **Avoid Dialysis** by Eating Tasty
and **Kidney-Friendly Food**

LACY HOLLAND

TABLE OF CONTENTS

Introduction

There are two kidneys in the human body. They're bean-shaped organs found at the back of the body, just below the rib cage on either side of the spine. Each kidney is about the size of a fist. The essential function of your kidneys is to cleanse (filter) the blood, expelling toxins (waste), extra salt, and water as urine. Waste may build up in the bloodstream and make you ill if the kidneys are compromised and don't work properly. Your kidneys contribute to the regulation of salt and mineral levels in the body, the production of blood pressure-regulating hormones, the formation of red blood cells, and the maintenance of bone health.

Kidney disease indicates that the kidneys have been impaired and are no longer performing as effectively as they should. Because kidney function worsens over time, kidney disease is considered to be «chronic.» Kidney failure, generally referred to as an end-stage renal disease, occurs due to kidney disease. At this point, you'll require dialysis (synthetic filtration) or a kidney transplant. There are five stages to kidney disease. The effectiveness with which the kidneys filter toxins and extra substances from the blood determines the stages. Kidney failure is divided into five stages, ranging from the normal (stage 1) to some of the most serious failures of the kidney (stage 5). Healthcare practitioners use the glomerular filtration rate to determine the stage of renal functioning (GFR). Chronic kidney disease (CKD) is no cure, although early management may help keep renal function at a higher level for longer. Absolute renal failure, if left unchecked, may result in death. Individuals with end-stage CKD have two options: dialysis or kidney transplantation. Depending on the reason for your kidney illness, you may be prescribed a variety of medicines.

A renal diet is a nutritional plan used to decrease the amount of waste in the bloodstream. The renal diet is designed to put as little strain as possible on the kidneys while providing the body with the energy and nutrition it requires. A renal diet follows a few fundamental guidelines. The first is that it should be a well-balanced, nutrient-dense, long-term diet rich in whole grains, vitamins, fibers, carbs, omega-3 fats, as well as fluids. Proteins may be adequate but not in excess. The amount of blood collected is reduced to a minimum level. Regularly, electrolyte levels in the blood are tested, and the diet is changed as needed. It's critical to fol-

low the doctor's as well as the dietician's recommendations.

Protein intake is necessary for everyday tissue repair but must be kept to a minimum level. Excess proteins must be broken down into nitrates and carbs by the body. The body does not use nitrates. Therefore, they must be excreted via the kidneys. Carbohydrates are essential nutrients that should be eaten in adequate amounts. Cooking should be the only time you use table salt. Overloading the kidneys with too much salt causes fluid retention.

Diet is an important part of CKD treatment, as it may help reduce the disease's development. Some nutrients help your kidneys work better, while others make them work harder. You may feel as though you're in uncharted terrain, and managing your demands may be challenging. All of the newest food do's and don'ts may be perplexing to you and your family at first; the latest dietary restrictions can be irritating. Finding simple, healthy CKD recipes to help patients manage the number of chemicals and fluids in the blood is one of the most common problems that kidney patients face. The goal of this book is to provide a solid foundation for eating flavorful foods and making appropriate dietary changes.

CHAPTER 1:
All about the Kidney Diseases

1.1 Function of Kidneys in the Human Body

The kidneys are two bean-shaped organs located on each side of the vertebral column, behind the ribs, and behind the belly. Each kidney is approximately the size of a hefty fist and is around 4-5 inches in length. The kidneys are in charge of filtering your blood. They eliminate waste, maintain the balance of body fluids, and maintain proper electrolyte levels. Every day, all of your blood flows through them many times. The kidneys filter the blood, removing waste substances that are harmful to the body, and regulate the salt and water balance according to the needs of our body. Waste is converted to urine, which accumulates in the kidney's pelvis, a funnel-shaped organ that empties into the bladder through a tube known as the ureter. Around a million microscopic filters called nephrons are found in each kidney. Just 10% of the kidneys may be functioning, yet you're not aware of any symptoms or issues. If a kidney's blood supply is cut off, it may fail in part or whole. Kidney failure may result as a result of this.

The kidneys are considered essential organs to guarantee the vital functions of our body. A little curiosity from the distant world of the ancient Egyptians suggests the importance that this ancient civilization already gave to these organs. In the art of mummification, characteristic of this people, before preserving a corpse, one of the few organs that they left in position was precisely the kidneys, which gives the idea that at that time they were considered of primary importance.

STRUCTURE OF KIDNEYS

Males and females have bean-shaped organs that weigh about 125-175 g and 115-155 g, correspondingly. The kidney usually measures 11-14 cm in length, 6 cm in width, and 4 cm in thickness. The kidneys are shielded by fat, muscles, and back ribs. The renal fat pad, also known as perirenal fat, shields the kidneys from excessive pressure. The renal hilum is a midline indentation on the kidneys that serves as the opening and closing point for structures like nerves, ureters, vessels, as well as lymphatics that fuel or empty the kidneys.

VASCULAR CIRCULATION

Blood proteins can recognize diabetics that are at the greatest risk of kidney impairment. A novel method of treating invasive kidney cancer is safe in a clinical study. Experts in the field of kidney disease believe it's a pastime to eliminate race from medical strategies. It is difficult to do so.

The renal arteries, which are important branches of the abdominal aorta, provide blood to the kidneys. These afferent arterioles ingress and split into many levels to create a highly specialized and homogeneous network of afferent arterioles, which subsequently form the glomeruli, which are specialized capillary beds. A glomerulus is one of the nephron's components. The efferent arterioles are formed as the capillaries recombine. They create a peritubular network surrounding the tubules in the external cortex. The peritubular system is substituted by lengthy straight branches termed the vasa recta in the interior third of the cortex and medulla. The filtered blood returns to the heart via the left and right renal veins, which drain into the inferior vena cava.

NEPHRONS

The functioning components of the kidneys are called nephrons, and each kidney has approximately 1.3 million of them. Tubules and corpuscles are the two major components of a nephron. The glomeruli are contained inside the cup-shaped corpuscles. Tubules are tiny tubes that run through the inner portion of the kidney and control the flow of chemicals into and out of the bloodstream. They are divided into three sections; the proximal convoluted tubule, the loop of Henle, and the distal convoluted tubule, which are divided by a U-shaped curve (like a hairpin).

OTHER PARTS

Underneath the renal capsule, the cortex is the external renal tissue. Particularly in comparison to the other sections of the kidney, it seems to be lighter in color. Here you'll find the renal corpuscles and also the proximal and distal convoluted tubules. It extends into the medulla, the innermost portion of the kidney, and divides it into three triangular sections known as renal pyramids.

The loops of Henle in the kidney structure of every renal tubule, and also the collecting ducts, are placed in the renal pyramids. The apex, and renal papilla, of each renal pyramid, opens. The urine that forms within the pyramids is gathered here by a structure known as the minor calyx. A large calyx is formed when many small calices come together. To access the renal pelvis, urine passes via the main calices. The pelvis in the structure is a funnel-shaped accumulating structure created by all of the main calices joining together. It transfers urine from the entire kidney towards the ureter, which starts at the pelvic-ureteric intersection where the pelvis finishes.

The Gerota's fascia is a fibrous tissue that surrounds the adrenal glands, which are situated above the kidneys. It secures the kidney to the back of the abdomen. The renal capsule, located immediately within the renal fat pad, is a layer of strong fibrous tissue that surrounds the kidney.

HOW DO THE KIDNEYS WORK?

One-fifth of the blood pumped by the heart is absorbed and filtered in your kidneys. Excess water, salt, minerals, and waste are excreted in the urine, which is restored to circulation as 'clean' blood. The kidney filters all of the blood in only 5 minutes, which means your kidneys can process all of the blood 288 times in 24 hours. Kidneys are hardworking organs that must be maintained in the best possible condition so that you can feel healthy and well enough. Whether you think you have kidney problems, have already been tested, or are in perfect health, it's critical to look after such bean-shaped filterers so that they can continue functioning properly.

FUNCTIONS OF KIDNEYS

The kidneys' fundamental purpose is to keep homeostasis. This means they maintain fluid levels, electrolyte balance, and other variables that make the body's internal environment constant and comforting. They serve a variety of purposes:

EXCRETION OF WASTE

The kidneys remove different waste substances, which are excreted in the urine. These eliminated compounds are mainly of two types:

- Urea; it is formed as a by-product of protein breakdown.
- Uric acid; it is formed as a by-product of the degradation of nucleic acids.

NUTRIENT RE-ABSORPTION

The kidneys' roles include waste removal, nutrient re-absorption, and pH balance maintenance. The kidneys in the body reabsorb nutrients from the bloodstream and then distribute them to the parts of the body where they may be most beneficial to health. They may reabsorb other substances to maintain stability.

Among the reabsorbed products are:

- Amino acids
- Glucose
- Sodium bicarbonate
- Water
- Phosphate
- Chloride, sodium, magnesium, and potassium ions

KEEPING PH STABLE

The optimum pH level in humans is 7.38-7.42. Below this line, the body enters an acidic condition, and above it, it enters an alkaline state. Proteins and enzymes deteriorate and cease to function outside of this range. This may be deadly in severe instances. The kidneys, as well as the lungs, assist in maintaining a constant pH inside the human body. This is accomplished by the lungs regulating the content of carbon dioxide.

The pH of the kidneys is controlled by two processes:

- Regenerating and reabsorbing bicarbonate from the urine: Bicarbonate assists in acid neutralizing. If the pH is acceptable, the kidneys may store it or discharge it if the acid levels increase.

- Hydrogen ions, and fixed acids, are ousted: Any acid that does not form as a consequence of carbon dioxide is referred to as a fixed or nonvolatile acid. They are the consequence of incomplete glucose, lipid, and protein metabolism. Lactic, sulfuric, as well as phosphoric acid, is among them.

OSMOLALITY MODULATION

Osmolality is a measurement of the body's electrolyte-water balance, or perhaps the proportion of fluid to minerals. Dehydration is the most significant reason for electrolyte imbalance.

When the osmolality of blood plasma rises, the hypothalamus inside the brain reacts by sending a message to the pituitary gland. This, in turn, causes the secretion of antidiuretic hormone (ADH).

The kidney undergoes a variety of alterations in reaction to ADH, including:

- Increasing the content of urine
- Enhancing water reabsorption

Reopening sections of the collecting duct that usually do not allow water to enter, letting water back into the body and storing urea in the renal medulla rather than emitting it when it takes in water.

BLOOD PRESSURE REGULATION

When required, the kidneys control blood pressure, although they are accountable for slower changes. They alter the fluid outside of cells to regulate long-term compression in the arteries. Extracellular fluid is the medical name for this fluid. These fluid alterations occur as a result of the secretion of angiotensin II, a vasoconstrictor. Vasoconstrictors are the hormones that constrict blood arteries. They collaborate with other processes to enhance the intake of sodium chloride or salt by the kidneys. This effectively expands the extracellular fluid segment and elevates blood pressure.

Excessive alcohol use, smoking, and obesity are all examples of factors that may harm the kidneys over time.

ACTIVE COMPOUND SECRETION

A variety of essential chemicals are released by the kidneys, including:

- **Erythropoietin:** It is a hormone that regulates erythropoiesis, or the formation of red blood cells. Although the liver generates erythropoietin, the kidneys are the primary producers in adults.
- **Renin:** This hormone regulates artery expansion as well as the amount of plasma (blood plasma), lymph, and interstitial fluid. Lymph is a fluid that includes white blood cells that participate in immune function, and interstitial fluid seems to be the major element of extracellular fluid.
- **Calcitriol:** It is a vitamin D metabolite that is hormonally active. It enhances both the quantity of calcium that the intestines might absorb and the quantity of phosphate that the kidney can reabsorb.

1.2 What Are Kidney Diseases?

At the bottom of the rib cage are two fist-sized structures called kidneys. One kidney is located on each side of the spine. Kidneys that are in good condition are essential for a healthy body. They remove waste, excess fluid, and other impurities from the bloodstream. Toxins are stored in the intestine and can be eliminated via urine. The kidneys also regulate the pH, salt, and potassium levels in the body. They produce hormones that control red blood cell formation and blood pressure. The kidneys even activate a form of vitamin D that helps calcium absorption.

In the United States, about 26 million individuals suffer from kidney disease. It occurs when your kidneys become weak and unable to function properly. Damage may be caused by diabetes, hypertension, and other chronic (long-term) diseases. Brittle bones, nerve damage, as well as malnutrition, are just a few of the side effects of kidney disease. If the disease develops, the kidneys may ultimately cease working altogether. This implies that dialysis would be necessary to complete the kidney's function. Dialysis is a proper intervention that cleans and purifies the blood with the help of a pump. It won't cure renal failure, but this will extend your life.

KIDNEY DISEASE SYMPTOMS

The kidneys are capable of responding to a wide range of circumstances. They will assist you in dealing with a few of the problems associated with renal diseases. As a consequence, the symptoms will emerge gradually if the kidney damage progresses. Indeed, symptoms do not emerge until the disease has worsened. You may have:

- High blood pressure
- Vomiting
- Nausea
- Appetite loss
- Metallic taste in the mouth
- Tiredness
- Fatigue
- Difficulty thinking
- Sleep issues
- Muscle cramps as well as spasms
- Swelling of the feet and ankles
- Tingling that doesn't seem to get away
- Breathlessness when fluid builds up in the lungs
- Chest pain as fluid accumulates over the heart's lining

1.3 Types of Kidney Diseases

CKD (CHRONIC KIDNEY DISEASE)

Chronic kidney disease is a condition that affects the kidneys. CKD is the most prevalent kind of kidney disease. This is an inflammatory condition that worsens with time. High blood pressure is a frequent reason. High blood pressure can put too much strain on the glomeruli in the kidneys, causing them to fail. Glomeruli are small blood arteries in the kidneys that purify the blood. The increasing pressure destroys these vessels with time, causing kidney function to deteriorate.

Kidney function will ultimately decline to the point that the kidneys will be unable to work efficiently. Dialysis would be required in this situation. Dialysis removes excess fluid and waste from the bloodstream. This is a treatment for renal illness, but it is not a cure. Depending on the circumstances, a kidney transplant might be a possibility.

Diabetes can significantly affect the development of chronic kidney disease. In fact, it has been extensively studied and shown that about one third of patients suffering from diabetes develop chronic kidney disease. This is a set of illnesses characterized by elevated blood sugar levels. Over time, excessive blood sugar levels destroy the blood vessels within the kidneys. This causes a reduction in the function of the kidneys, which are no longer able to filter the blood properly. When your body is overwhelmed with pollutants, kidney failure may develop. Chronic kidney disease affects 37 million individuals in the United States (CKD).

The phrase "chronic kidney disease" refers to long-term kidney impairment that may worsen over time. Your kidneys may cease functioning if the condition is severe. This is referred to as kidney failure or end-stage renal disease (ESRD). To survive if the kidneys are damaged, you will require dialysis or a kidney transplant.

WHAT CAUSES CKD?

CKD may affect anybody. Some individuals are at a greater hazard than others. Some factors that enhance your chances of developing CKD include:

- Diabetes
- Blood pressure that is too high (hypertension)
- Cardiovascular disease
- Having a kidney illness in your family
- Being African, Hispanic, Native American, or Asian
- Being above the age of 60

WHAT ARE THE SIGNS AND SYMPTOMS OF KIDNEY DISEASE?

If the kidneys are weakening, you might notice several of the symptoms listed:

- Itching
- Muscle spasms
- Vomiting & nausea
- Not in the mood to eat
- Swelling in the ankles and feet
- Excessively urine (pee) or insufficient urine
- Having difficulty catching your breath
- Sleeping problems

You may have several of the symptoms listed if your kidneys quit functioning abruptly (acute kidney failure):

- Pain in the abdomen (belly)
- Back pain
- Diarrhea
- Fever
- Nosebleeds
- Rash
- Vomiting

Experiencing some or all of the symptoms listed above may indicate serious kidney issues. If you experience any of these problems, you should see your doctor as soon as possible.

COMPLICATIONS OF CHRONIC KIDNEY DISEASE

Your kidneys assist in the proper function of your whole body. If you have CKD, you may have issues with the remainder of your body's function. Anemia, bone disease, cardiovascular disease, excessive potassium, high calcium, and fluid accumulation are all frequent consequences of CKD.

STAGES OF CHRONIC KIDNEY DISEASE

Chronic kidney disease (CKD) is a term that encompasses all 5 phases of kidney impairment, ranging from little damage in Stage 1 to total kidney failure in Stage 5. The phases of kidney disease are determined by the kidneys' ability to filter waste and excess fluid from the bloodstream.

The estimated glomerular filtration rate, or eGFR, is how clinicians determine how efficiently your kidneys filter wastes from the blood. Your eGFR is determined by a blood test for creatinine, a pollutant in the blood. The eGFR value determines the stage of kidney disease.

1. eGFR of 90 or more indicates stage 1 CKD. In this phase, there is a modest kidney damage.

An eGFR of 90 or above usually indicates that your kidneys are strong and functioning properly, but you have significant symptoms of renal impairment. Protein in the urine (pee) and physical damage to the kidneys are both signs of kidney disease. In stage 1 of CKD, there are actions you can correct, or implement, in your lifestyle that can reduce kidney damage:

- Keep your blood sugar monitored closely if you also have diabetes.
- Periodically measure blood pressure levels.
- Follow a healthy, varied and balanced diet, consulting with your doctor on which foods are most appropriate and which ones to avoid based on your current clinical condition.
- Absolutely abstain from smoking.
- Engage in regular physical activity for an average of 30 minutes, 5 days a week.
- Keep yourself in a normal weight condition.
- Consult a nephrologist (kidney specialist).

2. eGFR in Stage 2 CKD around 60-89. Moderate kidney damage occurs at this stage, however, an eGFR of 60-89 indicates that the kidneys are still functioning properly. Whether you have Stage 2 kidney problems, however, your eGFR is adequate, but you have additional indications of renal impairment. Protein in the urine or direct kidney damage are signs of ongoing kidney disease. At this stage, you can adopt a healthier lifestyle by following the directions recommended in the previous stage 1 in order to slow down the course of the disease and reduce the risk of other complications.

3. eGFR in stage 3 CKD 30-59. If you have stage 3 CKD, your eGFR is around 30-59.

An eGFR of 30-59 indicates that your kidneys have been damaged and are not performing as effectively as they should. Stage 3 is divided into two sections:

- If your eGFR is between 45 and 59, you're at stage 3a.
- If your eGFR is between 30 and 44, you're at stage 3b.

A substantial proportion of people with stage 3 kidney disease show no symptoms or signs. However, if there are signs and symptoms, these may include:

- The hands and feet are swollen.
- Back discomfort.
- More or less urinating (peeing) than usual.
- As waste accumulates in the body and the kidneys fail to function properly, you're more prone to develop a lot of health problems.
- The blood pressure is too high.
- Anemia; is a kind of blood disorder (a lower amount of red blood cells).
- The disease of the bones.

You can do the following to prevent the Stage 3 kidney problems from becoming worse:

- Keep your blood sugar monitored closely if you also have diabetes.
- Periodically measure blood pressure levels.
- Follow a healthy, varied and balanced diet, consulting with your doctor on which foods are most appropriate and which ones to avoid based on your current clinical condition.

- Absolutely abstain from smoking.
- Engage in regular physical activity for an average of 30 minutes, 5 days a week.
- Keep yourself in a normal weight condition.
- Consult a nephrologist (kidney specialist) to set up a therapy tailored to your needs in order to preserve kidney function as much as possible; it will also advise you on how often to carry out tests and checks on your kidneys.
- Meet with a nutritionist who can assist you in maintaining a healthy diet.

If you do have diabetes or elevated blood pressure, talk to your doctor about ACE inhibitors and ARBs, which are blood pressure medications. These medications may sometimes help prevent the renal disease from worsening.

4. eGFR in stage 4 CKD 15-29. If you have stage 4 CKD, your eGFR is around 15-29.

If the eGFR is between 15 and 30, the kidneys are mildly or seriously impaired and not functioning properly. Stage 4 renal disease should be treated carefully since it is the last phase before kidney failure.

Many individuals with stage 4 renal disease have signs such as:

- The hands and feet are swollen.
- Back discomfort.
- More or less urinating (peeing) than usual.
- As waste accumulates in the body and the kidneys fail to function properly, you may likely have a lot of health problems at Stage 4.
- The blood pressure is too high.
- Anemia; is a kind of blood disorder (a lower amount of red blood cells).
- The disease of the bones.

Your doctor will advise you to do the following to prevent kidney disease from worsening at this stage:

- Consult with a nephrologist (renal specialist) regularly, who will plan a suitable treatment protocol and advise you on how often your kidneys should be examined. Also, meet with a nutritionist, who will assist you in maintaining a balanced diet.
- If your doctor recommends it, use blood pressure medications such as ACE inhibitors as well as ARBs. These medications may occasionally help prevent kidney disease from worsening if you do have diabetes or elevated blood pressure.
- This is the moment to start talking to the nephrologist on how to brace for renal failure if you have stage 4 kidney disease. To survive once your kidneys fail, you'll need to begin dialysis or get a kidney transplant.

Preparation for dialysis: When the kidneys fail, dialysis cleans your blood. There are several factors to take into account such as the type of dialysis, the weekly schedule of treatments and the impact they will have on your daily life.

Getting ready for a transplant: Kidney transplant is a surgery to replace a diseased and / or severely damaged kidney with a healthy one from another person. You might not have to begin dialysis at all if you can identify a healthy kidney donor. When kidney function is severely impaired, you may be considered a suitable candidate for transplant.

5. eGFR in stage 5 CKD less than 15. If you have chronic kidney disease that is irreversibly stage 5, your eGFR will be less than 15. Waste accumulates in the blood when the kidneys fail, making you extremely ill.

Here are some of the symptoms and signs suggestive of ongoing renal failure:

- Persistent itching and dry skin
- Muscle cramps
- Nausea, vomiting, and loss of appetite
- Swelling in the hands, feet, and ankles
- Decrease in the amount of urine, which is foamy
- Frequent urination and often with the presence of blood
- Constant fatigue
- Mental confusion
- Sleep disorders

To survive once your kidneys fail, you'll need to begin dialysis or get a kidney transplant.

STONES IN THE KIDNEYS

Another frequent kidney problem is kidney stones. They become solid masses once minerals and other chemicals are in the blood and congeal in the kidneys (stones). Kidney stones are typically passed through the body via urine. These stones may be very painful to pass, although they seldom cause serious complications.

GLOMERULONEPHRITIS

Glomerulonephritis is a condition in which the glomeruli become inflamed. The glomeruli are small structures in the kidneys that filter blood. Certain medications, infections, and birth defects can cause inflammation at this level known as glomerulonephritis. This problem usually tends to resolve itself.

POLYCYSTIC KIDNEY DISEASE- PKD

Polycystic kidney disease is a hereditary condition in which the kidneys develop many cysts (small sacs of fluid). If these cysts interfere with, and compromise, kidney function, they can lead to kidney failure. (It's worth noting that particular kidney cysts are really very common and almost generally benign.) Polycystic kidney disease, on the other hand, is a different, more severe ailment.

INFECTIONS OF THE URINARY TRACT

Urinary tract infections (UTIs) are infectious diseases of the urinary tract that may affect any part of the body. The most frequent infections are those of the bladder and urethra. They are readily treated and seldom result in further health issues. These infections may proceed to the kidneys and cause renal failure if it goes unchecked.

1.4 Diagnosis of Kidney Diseases

Your physician will first assess if you fall into one of the high-risk categories. They will next do some tests to check whether your kidneys are in good working order. This type of assessment may include exams such as:

GLOMERULAR FILTRATION RATE (GFR)

This test will identify the stage of renal disease and how effectively your kidneys are functioning.

ULTRASOUND OR COMPUTERIZED TOMOGRAPHY (CT SCAN)

Your kidneys, as well as your urinary system, may be seen clearly with ultrasounds and CT scans. Your doctor may use the images to determine if the kidneys are too tiny or too massive. They may also reveal any cancers or structural issues that could exist.

A BIOPSY OF THE KIDNEY IS PERFORMED

While you're anesthetized, your doctor will take a tiny bit of tissue from the kidney throughout a kidney biopsy. Your doctor may use the tissue sample to identify the kind of renal disease you have and the extent of the damage.

URINE EXAMINATION

A urine sample may be requested by your doctor to check for albumin. When the kidneys are impaired, albumin is a substance that may be transferred into your urine.

CREATININE LEVEL IN THE BLOOD

Creatinine is a byproduct. When creatine (a chemical held in muscle) is decomposed, it is released into the bloodstream. If your kidneys aren't performing as expected, the amount of creatinine in the blood will rise.

WHAT IS THE TREATMENT FOR KIDNEY DISEASE?

Kidney disease treatment generally focuses on addressing the illness's underlying cause. This means that your doctor will work with you to improve the way you control your blood pressure, blood sugar, as well as cholesterol levels. To treat renal disease, they may use several of the following methods.

MEDICATION AND DRUGS

Angiotensin-converting enzyme (ACE) inhibitors, like lisinopril as well as ramipril/angiotensin receptor blockers (ARBs), like irbesartan and olmesartan, will be prescribed by your doctor. Those are all blood pressure medicines that may help renal disease develop more slowly. Even if you don't have high blood pressure, your doctor may recommend these medicines to help you maintain kidney function.

Cholesterol medications may also be used to help you (such as simvastatin). These medicines may help preserve kidney function by lowering blood cholesterol levels. Your doctor may also prescribe medications to reduce swelling and treat anemia based on your symptoms (reduction in the number of red blood cells).

CHANGES IN DIET AND LIFESTYLE

It's just as essential to make dietary adjustments as it is to take medicine. Several of the underlying reasons for kidney disease may be avoided by following a healthy lifestyle. Your doctor may advise you to:

- Insulin injections for diabetic patients.
- Limit your intake of high-cholesterol foods.
- Reduce your sodium intake.
- Begin eating a heart-healthy diet rich in fresh fruits and vegetables, whole grains, as well as low-fat dairy products.
- Minimize your alcohol intake.
- Give up smoking.
- Boost your physical activity.
- Weight loss.

WHAT CAN BE DONE TO AVOID KIDNEY DISEASE?

Certain kidney disease risk factors, such as age, ethnicity, or family history, are uncontrollable. However, there are some things you may do to help avoid kidney disease:

CONSUME LOTS OF WATER

- If you have diabetes, keep your blood sugar and blood pressure under control.
- Reduce your salt consumption and stop smoking.
- Be careful while using over-the-counter medications.
- For over-the-counter medicines, always follow the dose recommendations. Kidney damage may be caused by having excess aspirin (Bayer) and ibuprofen (Advil, Motrin). If the usual dosages of these medicines aren't managing your pain, see your doctor.

EXAMINE YOURSELF

Request a blood test for renal issues from your doctor. Kidney issues usually don't show symptoms until they've progressed. A basic metabolic panel (BMP) is a common blood test that may be performed as part of a regular medical examination. It looks for creatinine, as well as urea in your blood. When the kidneys are not functioning properly, chemicals seep into the bloodstream. A BMP may identify kidney issues early on when they are more manageable. If you have diabetes, cardiovascular disease, or hypertension, you should be checked every year.

CERTAIN FOODS SHOULD BE AVOIDED

Certain substances in your diet may have a role in the formation of kidney stones. These are some of them:

Oxalate is a substance found in beets, greens, sweet potatoes, and chocolate. Excessive sodium animal protein, including beef and poultry. Citric acid is present in citrus fruits like oranges, lemons, and grapefruits.

1.5 Slow Down the Kidney Diseases

Working your kidneys, even if just a little, can make you feel better and help you live longer. You may postpone the need for renal failure therapy if you could somehow slow down your CKD. Changes you make to assist the heart, or the rest of the body will also benefit your kidneys. Here are a few things you may do to safeguard your kidneys or avoid doing:

- **Maintain a healthy blood sugar level.** Blood vessels, particularly the nephrons in the kidneys, are harmed by high blood sugar. Whether you have diabetes, the doctor will determine a fasting blood sugar target for you as well as a target for 2 hours once you eat. Check your blood sugar levels often to observe how they fluctuate depending on what you eat and how engaged you are. If you have not already, reduce your intake of added sugars and processed carbohydrates like bread, cakes, and rice. Take walks or engage in other forms of physical activity. Take your diabetic medication(s) exactly as directed.

- **Maintain the blood pressure in the expected range prescribed by your doctor.** Even if the blood pressure has always been moderate, it may suddenly be high, and difficult to manage. It is common for people with CKD to need several blood pressure medications. At home, you can monitor your blood pressure. Keep track of your readings so you can inform your doctor when your blood pressure is high or low and when you consume your blood pressure medications. If you are experiencing adverse effects, speak with your doctor; a different medication may be better for you. Exercise may also benefit in the reduction of blood pressure.

- **If you are overweight, you should lose weight.** The CARDIA research of young individuals (average age 35) over 10 years demonstrated that the more persons weighed, the quicker their kidney function deteriorated. Even if individuals did not have diabetes or elevated blood pressure, this was true. It is difficult to reduce weight, but it is possible, and numerous methods may be used. If you need assistance, ask your care team for assistance.

- **Soda should not be consumed.** Drinking one or maybe more normal sodas per day has been related to kidney impairment in major research. The second major research discovered that drinking two or even more diet sodas per day might cause kidney damage or hasten it.

- **Whether you smoke or use illegal drugs, make an effort to quit.** The kidneys are harmed by smoking and most illicit drugs. Naturally, if quitting were simple, everyone would be doing it. There are many methods for quitting smoking, including cold turkey, patches, nicotine gum, and e-cigarettes. Even reducing back may be beneficial. If you take street drugs, you might need some treatment. If you need assistance quitting an addiction that is causing you damage, talk to your healthcare provider.

- **Maintain a healthy pH level in your blood.** The pH of your blood should be between 7.38 and 7.42. When your kidneys aren't working properly, they can't maintain the acid-base ratio in your body in control. The acid may build up in your body as a result of eating protein-rich meals. Grains, as well as protein foods such as meat, eggs, milk products, beans, and peas, break down into acid wastes. Protein is required by the organism for muscle repair and self–healing. However, most of us consume more proteins than we require. One method to help your kidneys survive longer, especially if you're older, is to eat low-acid food (with plenty of vegetables). Discuss with your doctor if sodium bicarbonate may also help sustain your kidneys. It is extremely low cost and comes in tablet form.

- **Reduce your protein intake.** Blood urea nitrogen is formed when protein is broken down (BUN). The kidneys have a difficult time removing BUN. When you consume less protein, you produce less BUN, which may extend the life of your kidneys. According to research, eating a very low protein diet may assist even more, and this is difficult to do, so there is a possibility of malnutrition.

- **Phosphorus should be used in proportion.** Meat, chicken, fish, milk products, nuts, lentils, beans, and cola drinks all contain phosphorus. Your kidneys aren't removing excess phosphorus from the blood as they should be. Your bones may become weak if the levels are too high.

- **Shellfish should be eaten in moderation.** In mice, researchers discovered that a toxin termed domoic acid present in shellfish and certain fish that consume algae may damage the kidneys. Human beings are not mice. The most alarming discovery was that even extremely low amounts of the toxin might damage the kidneys. Purines are abundant in shellfish, which may be problematic if you do have gout. So, if you consume a lot of shellfish, it may be a good idea to cut it down.

- **Don't eat canned foods.** Bisphenol A is used to coat the majority of foodstuff cans in the United States (BPA). Hypertension, diabetes, as well as obesity, have all been related to BPA. Numerous canned foods are rich in salt or sugar and heavily processed. BPA is absent in products stored in long-life cartons or glass jars.

- **Certain pain relievers should be avoided.** NSAIDs (non-steroidal anti-inflammatory drugs) may harm the kidneys. The kidneys need a regular blood supply to function optimally. Blood flow into & out of the kidneys is reduced by NSAIDs. In most situations, NSAIDs induce CKD after years of regular usage. However, once CKD has developed, NSAIDs may hasten its progression. Consult your doctor about pain relief alternatives that aren't harmful to your kidneys. If you take one pill now and then and your kidneys are still working, follow it up with a large glass of water.

- **Antioxidants could be beneficial.** Each cell in the body demands oxygen to function properly. However, excessive oxygen in improper areas may cause damage, similar to rust. Antioxidants protect the cells and may also benefit your kidneys. Consult your doctor to see whether antioxidants like these are beneficial.

- **Fish oil.** This may help reduce the progression of CKD caused by IgA nephropathy.
- **Get Moving.** Cardiovascular disease and stroke are also linked to CKD. Diseases that affect the kidneys can affect the heart and blood vessels as well. The good news is that exercising gets your blood flowing, which benefits your heart and kidneys by increasing blood flow. As a result, the workout is a win-win situation for the body. It may potentially delay the progression of CKD.
- **Every day, aim for 30 minutes of physical movement.** The 30 minutes shouldn't complete in one sitting. If you want, you may divide your workout into 10–minute halves. Are you thinking of beginning a fitness routine? If it's been a long time since you've exercised, see your doctor first. Begin gently and gradually increase time, distance, and weight. Keep track of your progress to see how you're progressing. You may even establish objectives for yourself and praise yourself when you achieve them. Exercise doesn't have to consist of a boring run on a treadmill at a high-priced gym. Here are some additional ideas to consider, and you may come up with much more on your own:
- **Walking is excellent exercise,** but if you walk with a companion, you may spend time together as well. You may go for a stroll outside when the weather is better, and you reside in a safe area. Alternatively, many individuals walk at malls or at interior tracks to avoid missing out. You'll get more intensive exercise if you jog-walk (alternating between jogging and walking).
- **Pick a sport to participate in.** If you like a team activity, such as bowling, tennis, and badminton, you may spend time with people while also improving your fitness.
- **Put forth some effort.** Make fencing or a wall out of paint. Pick a few weeds or cut the bushes in the garden. Use a push mower to mow the grass. Vacuum a few of the rooms. You'll do something, feel good about yourself, and also be active as a result.
- **Dance, skate, and have fun.** Moving is moving, whether you're jumping on a trampoline, paddling a boat, or taking your lover for a spin. Consider what you enjoyed as a child; it may inspire you to attempt new things.

CHAPTER 2:
All about the Renal Diet?

2.1 What Is a Renal Diet?

A renal diet is an eating regimen used to help decrease the number of waste products in the blood. The renal diet is designed to put as little strain on the kidneys as possible while still providing the body with the energy and nutrition it requires. A renal diet is based on a few funda-mental concepts.

To reduce the quantity of waste in the blood, individuals with impaired kidney function must follow a renal or kidney diet. Waste products in the blood are caused by the consumption of food and drinks. If the kidneys are no longer able to function optimally, they cannot effectively filter the blood and eliminate waste products from the body. When waste accumulates in the blood, it may have a detrimental impact on a patient's electrolyte balance. A kidney diet can help improve kidney function and delay the development of related complications and total kidney failure.

A diet specifically formulated for the kidneys must have specific requirements, the most important of which are low in sodium, phosphorus, potassium, and protein. This diet also accentuates the necessity of eating high-quality protein and, in most cases, minimizing fluids. Some individuals may additionally need potassium and calcium restrictions. Because each person's body is unique, each patient must collaborate with a renal nutritionist to develop a diet customized to the patient's requirements. The following are a few substances that must be monitored to support a renal diet:

SODIUM

What do you know about sodium, and what function does it play in the body?

Sodium is a substance that may be found in a variety of natural foods. Most people consider salt and sodium to be interchangeable. Salt, on the other hand, is a sodium chloride substance. Foods that we consume may include salt or sodium in different ways. Because of the additional salt, processed foods typically have greater sodium levels. Sodium is among the three electrolytes that make up the human body (The other two include potassium and chloride). Electrolytes control the regulation of fluids inside and outside of the human body's tissues and cells. The following are some of the processes that sodium is engaged in:

- Keeping blood pressure and blood volume in check.
- Both nerve function and muscle contraction are regulated.
- Keeping the blood's acidic-base stability in check.
- Keeping a balance between how much liquid the body retains and how much it detoxifies.

Why should renal patients keep a close eye on their salt intake?

For individuals with renal illness, too much salt may be hazardous as their kidneys are incapable of properly removing excess sodium and liquid from the body. The accumulation of salt and fluid in the tissues, as well as circulation, may lead to:

- Thirst for water.
- Congestion in the legs, hands, as well as face, is known as edema.
- The blood pressure is too high.
- The surplus liquid in the blood may cause the heart to overstrain, triggering it to develop enlarged and feeble.
- Difficulty breathing: fluid may accumulate in the lungs, rendering the breath process harder.

How can patients keep track of their salt consumption?

- Always read the labels on foods. The amount of sodium in a given food is always reported.
- Keep an eye on the serving portions.
- Fresh meats should be used instead of processed meats.

- Fresh vegetables and fruits, as well as frozen foods with no added salt, are good choices to bring to the table every day.
- Avoid foods that have undergone numerous transformations.
- Always read labels and choose products with low sodium content.
- Use spices to flavor foods.
- When cooking at home, avoid adding salt. Limit salt intake to 400 mg each meal plus 150 mg every snack.

POTASSIUM

What is potassium, and what function does it play in the human body?

It is a mineral that may be found in several foods and the human body. This substance helps maintain the heartbeat steady and the muscles in good functioning order. Potassium is also required to maintain the bloodstream's fluid and electrolyte balance. The kidneys aid in maintaining a healthy potassium balance in the body by excreting excess potassium into the urine.

Why is it important for renal patients to keep track of their potassium intake?

Whenever the kidneys are damaged, the body's potassium levels rise because the kidneys are unable to eliminate extra potassium. Hyperkalemia is a condition in which there is too much potassium in the blood, which may lead to:

- Muscle deterioration

- An erratic heartbeat
- A weak pulse
- Heart attacks
- Death

How can patients keep track of their potassium consumption?

Once the kidneys are unable to sustain potassium, it is necessary to monitor the amount of potassium entering the body.

Follow these guidelines to maintain optimal, and safe, blood potassium levels:

- Consult a renal dietician to create a personalized meal plan.
- Avoid foods rich in potassium.
- Limit to a maximum of 8 oz. the daily consumption of milk and derivatives.
- Vegetables and fruit are always the foods to be favored.
- Avoid potassium-containing spices and salt substitutes.
- Avoid products containing potassium chloride (read the product label).
- Do not eat excessively large meals.

PHOSPHORUS

What is Phosphorus, and what function does it play in the human body?

Phosphorus is an important mineral for bone health and growth. This substance is also important for the formation of connective tissue, as well as when phosphorus-rich food is eaten and digested; the phosphorus is absorbed by the small intestines and deposited in the bones.

Why is it important for renal patients to keep track of their Phosphorus intake?

Excessive phosphorus in the blood may be removed by normal functioning kidneys. If kidney function is impaired, the kidneys cannot get rid of excess phosphorus in the body. High levels of phosphorus can cause various problems such as the loss of calcium from the bones, which become brittle and with a greater risk of fracture. This also causes harmful calcium deposits in blood vessels, lungs, eyes, as well as heart.

How can patients keep track of their Phosphorus consumption?

Phosphorus is present in a variety of foods. As a result, individuals with impaired kidney function should see a renal dietician to assist them in controlling their phosphorus levels.

Tips for keeping phosphorus levels in check:

- Learn which foods have a reduced phosphorus content.
- Keep a careful eye on the serving size.
- At snacks and meals, consume smaller amounts of high-protein foods.
- Fresh fruits and veggies should be consumed.
- Consult your doctor regarding the use of phosphate binders at mealtime.
- Phosphorus-fortified packaged foods should be avoided. On ingredient labels, look for phosphorus or keywords that start with the letter "PHOS."
- Keep a diet journal.

PROTEIN

Protein is not an issue for kidneys that are in good condition. This is normally eaten, while waste products are produced, which are processed by the kidney's nephrons. The waste is converted to urine with the assistance of extra renal proteins. Damaged kidneys, on the other hand, fail to eliminate protein waste, which builds up in the blood.

Protein intake is difficult for CKD patients since the quantity varies depending on the stage of the disease. Protein is necessary for tissue upkeep and other physiological functions; therefore, follow your nephrologist's or renal dietician's recommendations for your particular stage of illness.

FLUIDS

Fluid management is critical for patients with chronic kidney disease in the latter stages since normal fluid intake may lead to fluid buildup in the body, which can be hazardous. Because dialysis patients often have reduced urine production, an increase in liquid in the body may impose undue strain on the heart and lungs.

The fluid allowance for each patient is determined on a personal level, based on urine output and dialysis conditions. It is essential to carefully follow the recommendations on fluid consumption given by the nephrologist or dietician.

To keep their fluid consumption under control, patients should:

- Drink just as much as your doctor prescribes.
- Count all products that will thaw at ambient

temperature (such as Jell-O® and popsicles).

- Keep track of the number of liquids you use while cooking.

2.2 Foods to Consume and Avoid During Renal/Kidney Diet

The kidneys are organs that are bean-like and perform many different functions. Filtering the blood, eliminating waste substances through urine formation, generating hormones, regulating minerals, and maintaining fluid balance are all functions of the kidneys.

Kidney disease is caused by several factors and causes, some of which are: uncontrolled diabetes, excessive blood pressure, alcoholism, cardiovascular disease, HIV, and hepatitis C. Fluid may accumulate in the body and waste in the bloodstream when the kidneys get damaged and cannot work properly.

However, consuming or restricting certain foods from your diet may assist in reducing waste product buildup in the blood, enhance kidney function, as well as prevent future damage. If you have renal disease, here are ten things to consume or avoid:

FOODS TO CONSUME

- **Red bell peppers:** Low in potassium and rich in taste, red bell peppers are indeed a great dietary choice for those with renal disease.

They are rich in vitamin A, vitamin C, vitamin B6, fiber, and folic acid. It is a very versatile food because it can be eaten raw as a snack with a sauce, diced and stir-fried, or roasted and added to a sandwich. The possibilities are limitless. Cabbage, cauliflower, kale, spinach, as well as sweet potatoes are some vegetables good for kidney health.

- **Blueberries:** They are often regarded as a "superfood" with good reason. Blueberries are high in antioxidants and a limited calorie source of fiber and vitamin C. Bring them home when they're in abundance at the local grocery store or supermarket. During the off-season, or if you want to make it easier to put them into a smoothie, you may buy frozen berries. Strawberries, cranberries, and raspberries are other excellent foods to consume if you have a renal disease for variation.

- **Garlic:** If you're accustomed to eating foods that are high in additives like salt, you may assume that converting to a kidney-friendly food would be bland, but it doesn't have to be. Garlic is an excellent method to enhance the taste of the food. This fantastic vegetable also helps remove plaque, and reduce cholesterol, inflammation, and blood pressure. As far as the method of use is concerned, the fresh one is preferable, but if it is not possible, even garlic powder can be acceptable. Make sure you stay away from the garlic salt.

- **Egg whites:** Protein is the body's building component. However, it must be eaten with caution and in moderation by renal disease sufferers. Egg whites contain little phosphorus instead of other protein sources and provide all necessary amino acids. If you want to obtain protein from meat, go for omega-3-rich seafood like salmon and lean cuts of meat (red) like loin and round.

- **Onions:** Onions are another excellent method to add flavor to any dish, and they also offer health advantages. They're low in potassium but high in flavonoids, a strong antioxidant that may help prevent cancer and cardiovascular disease. Onions are also high in chromium, a mineral that has been shown to help the body better absorb carbs, fats, and proteins.

FOODS TO AVOID

- **Soda:** They're loaded with sugar and calories, and preservatives to prolong shelf life and prevent deterioration. Phosphorus, an ingredient that is easily absorbed by the body, is abundant in dark-colored soft drinks.
- **Avocados:** They are often lauded for their health advantages, so you may be shocked to learn that they're on the list of foods to avoid. They are high in potassium, which many renal patients might have to restrict, in addition to beneficial fats, fiber, and antioxidants.
- **Foods in cans:** The accessibility of canned goods, from veggies to soups and beans, is difficult to refute. However, the longer shelf

life which these products provide comes at a cost. Because salt is frequently used to maintain these products, they are rich in sodium. If you have to buy canned goods, look for ones that have "no salt added."

- **Dairy:** Although milk and its derivatives are rich in nutrients and vitamins, their high content of phosphorus, potassium, and proteins makes them potentially harmful foods in certain quantities for those suffering from kidney disease. They would be Ok on their own, but when coupled with other phosphorus-rich meals, the results may be disastrous. Excessive phosphorus intake may create an accumulation of phosphorus in the bloodstream when the kidneys are impaired, according to research. This may thin and weaken your bones over time, increasing the danger of bone-breaking or fracture.
- **Meats that have been processed:** If you're noticing a tendency here, it's because there is one. Products that are being processed or made to be shelf-stable for long periods but would otherwise perish in their natural form should be avoided. Processed meats have usually been salted, dried, cured, and even canned, resulting in high sodium meals like hot dogs, bacon, pepperoni, jerky, as well as sausage. These meals are also rich in protein, which is another aspect of the diet to keep an eye on if you have renal disease.

CONCLUSION

Whether you have renal disease or not, what you consume has an impact on your health.

Managing your blood pressure and blood sugar requires maintaining a good weight and eating a well-balanced diet. Higher blood pressure and diabetes, as well as a variety of other diseases, such as cardiovascular disease, heart attacks, and stroke, are two of the main causes of kidney disease.

It's more about portion management and finding the proper mix of protein, fats, and carbs to ensure you're getting sufficient calories and nutrients in a kidney-healthy diet than it is about eliminating products.

CHAPTER 3:
Delicious Renal Diet Recipes for Breakfast

RED MUESLI WITH CRANBERRIES

SERVINGS: 8

PREPARATION TIME: 10 minutes

Ingredients:

> 1/2 cup (125 g) soy or rice yogurt
> 1/2 cup (115 ml) cranberry juice with no added sugar
> 6 tbsp. old-fashioned rolled oats
> 2 tbsp. dried cranberries
> 1 tbsp. sunflower seeds without added salt
> 1 tbsp. wheat germ
> 2 tsp. honey
> 1/4 tsp. vanilla extract
> 1/2 tsp. fine salt

Directions:

1. Mix the old-fashioned oats, yogurt, dried cranberries, sunflower seeds, wheat germ, honey, vanilla, salt, and cranberry juice in a medium bowl.

2. Cover the bowl and refrigerate for a minimum of 8 hours and no longer than 1 day.

NUTRITIONAL VALUES:

Sodium: 189 mg

Potassium: 325 mg

Phosphorus: 247 mg

Protein: 7 g

Carbs: 40 g

Fat: 5 g

CREAMY APPLE OATS

SERVINGS: 4

PREPARATION TIME: 45 minutes

Ingredients:

> 4 apples the Pink Lady or Jazz type
> 1 cup (80 g) steel-cut oats
> 4 cups (1 L) water
> 3 tbsp. brown sugar
> 1/2 tsp. ground cinnamon
> Pinch of fine salt
> 1/2 cup (125 g) soy yogurt

Directions:

1. Take 2 apples and grate them through the large holes of a grater (avoid the core).
2. Take a large enough saucepan and heat it over medium-high heat.
3. Place the oats in the hot pot (without water) and lightly toast it for about 2 minutes.
4. Add the grated apples and the water bringing it to a boil at this point reduce the heat, keep the water to a boil, and mix for about 10 minutes.
5. Meanwhile, cut the other 2 apples into small pieces.
6. As soon as the oats are cooked for 10 minutes, add the remaining 2 apples, the cinnamon powder, the sugar, and the salt.
7. Then cook for about 15 minutes, stirring occasionally, until the oats become thicker and the apples become soft.
8. Enter the oats with apples in 4 servings and drizzle with 2 tablespoons of soy yogurt and 3 teaspoons of brown sugar.

NUTRITIONAL VALUES:

Sodium: 149 mg

Potassium: 271 mg

Phosphorus: 137 mg

Protein: 5 g

Carbs: 41 g

Fat: 3 g

STUFFED BISCUITS WITH BACON AND TOFU

SERVINGS: 12

PREPARATION TIME: 35 minutes

Ingredients:

> 2 cups (240 g) flour
> 1 tbsp. honey
> 1/2 tsp. baking soda
> 1 tsp. lemon juice
> 8 tbsp. extra-virgin olive oil
> 3/4 cup (175 ml) unsweetened and unforti-fied soy milk

Stuffing:

> 4 medium eggs
> 8 oz. (225 g) low-sodium bacon, of which 1 ¼ ounce (35 g) diced
> 1 cup (250 g) grated or shredded extra-firm tofu
> 1/4 cup (25 g) finely sliced scallions

Directions:

1. Preheat the oven to 425ºF.

Prepare the stuffing as follows:

2. Scramble the underdone eggs slightly.
3. Crisp up the bacon in a skillet.
4. Combine all 4 ingredients in a mixing bowl and put them aside.

Prepare the dough as follows:

5. Mix all dry ingredients in a large mixing bowl.
6. Make a well in the middle of the mixture and add the soy milk, honey, lemon juice and the remaining ingredients. Stir well.
7. Use a muffin pan liner or gently oil and flour the base and sides of the muffin tins.
8. Fill muffin tins with 1/4 cup of batter.
9. Preheat the oven to 425ºF and bake for 10-12 minutes, or until lightly browned.

NUTRITIONAL VALUES:

Sodium: 301 mg

Potassium: 147 mg

Phosphorus: 166 mg

Protein: 10 g

Carbs: 19 g

Fat: 21 g

CREAMY BLUEBERRY OATS

SERVINGS: 1

PREPARATION TIME: 15 minutes

Ingredients:

> 1/3 cup (35 g) old-fashioned rolled oats
> 1/3 cup (90 g) soy yogurt
> 1/2 cup (125 ml) unsweetened and unforti-fied soy milk
> 2/3 cup (100 g) fresh or frozen blueberries
> 1 tablespoon chia seeds
> 1/2 teaspoon vanilla extract
> 1/2 tablespoon maple syrup

Directions:

1. Mix all the ingredients in the container you want to have breakfast in.
2. Leave to rest in the fridge for 8-12 hours (1 night) and finally enjoy breakfast.

NUTRITIONAL VALUES:

Sodium: 124 mg

Potassium: 454 mg

Phosphorus: 297 mg

Protein: 7 g

Carbs: 48 g

Fat: 6 g

SPICY RED AND GREEN PEPPER TOFU

SERVINGS: 2

PREPARATION TIME: 20 minutes

Ingredients:

> 1 tsp. extra-virgin olive oil
> 1/4 cup (25 g) diced red bell pepper
> 1/4 cup (25 g) diced green bell pepper
> 1 cup (250 g) tofu, firm (pick less than 10 percent calcium)
> 1 tsp. powdered onion
> 1/4 tsp. powdered garlic
> 1 garlic clove, chopped
> 1/8 tsp. turmeric

Directions:

1. Cook garlic and both bell peppers in extra-virgin olive oil in a moderate non-stick pan.
2. Toss the tofu into the skillet once it has been rinsed and drained. Combine the rest of the ingredients and stir well.
3. Cook, occasionally stirring, until the tofu has become a little golden brown, approximately 20 minutes. The water in the mixture will evaporate.
4. Tofu scrambler should be served warm.

NUTRITIONAL VALUES:

Sodium: 23 mg

Potassium: 466 mg

Phosphorus: 241 mg

Protein: 17 g

Carbs: 9 g

Fat: 12 g

CREAMY CINNAMON OATS

SERVINGS: 5

PREPARATION TIME: 5 minutes

Ingredients:

> 2 ½ cups (200 g) old-fashioned rolled oats
> 2 ½ cups (590 ml) unfortified and unsweetened coconut milk
> 8 tsp. honey
> 2 ½ tsp. vanilla extract
> 1 ¼ tsp. ground cinnamon
> Pinch of fine salt

Directions:

1. Combine old-fashioned oats, coconut milk, honey, vanilla, cinnamon, and salt in a large enough bowl.
2. Divide the resulting mixture into 5 (8-ounce) jars.
3. Screw the lids of the jars, keeping them in the refrigerator overnight and for no more than 5 days.
4. If desired, at the time of consumption, you can add a little cranberry.

NUTRITIONAL VALUES:

Sodium: 161 mg

Potassium: 238mg

Phosphorus: 177 mg

Protein: 6 g

Carbs: 25 g

Fat: 4 g

BLUEBERRY OAT CAKES

SERVINGS: 6

PREPARATION TIME: 20 minutes

Ingredients:

› 2 ½ cups (200 g) old-fashioned rolled oats
› 1 ½ cup (350 ml) unsweetened and unenriched rice milk
› 1 egg, lightly beaten
› 1/3 cup (75 g) pure maple syrup
› 2 tbsp. canola oil
› 1 tsp. vanilla extract
› 1 tsp. ground cinnamon
› 1 tsp. baking powder
› Pinch of fine salt
› 3/4 cup (115 g) frozen or fresh blueberries

Directions:

1. Combine the oats and rice milk in a large enough bowl.
2. Let it soak, cover the bowl, and let it rest in the refrigerator for about 8-12 hours until most of the liquid is absorbed.
3. Once the mixture is ready, preheat the oven to 375ºF.
4. Get 12 non-stick muffin tins and coat them with cooking spray.
5. Combine the oat mixture with maple syrup, canola oil, egg, vanilla, cinnamon, baking powder, and fine salt. Mix well.
6. Fill the muffin cups with the mixture obtained for about 1/4 of their capacity.
7. Add 1 tablespoon of blueberries to each cup.
8. Cook the oat cakes for about 25-30 minutes.
9. Once cooked, let them cool for 10 minutes and remove them with the help of a kitchen knife. It is preferable to serve them still hot.
10. Keep them in the refrigerator for up to a couple of days by wrapping them hermetically. It is also possible to freeze them for up to 3 months.

NUTRITIONAL VALUES:

Sodium: 220 mg

Potassium: 279 mg

Phosphorus: 232 mg

Protein: 7 g

Carbs: 41 g

Fat: 8 g

PURPLE MUFFINS

SERVINGS: 12

PREPARATION TIME: 40 minutes

Ingredients:

› 1/2 cup (125 g) of soy yogurt
› 1 cup (200 g) sugar
› 2 medium eggs
› 2 cups (470 ml) unsweetened and unfortified soy milk
› 2 cups (240 g) all-purpose flour
› 2 tsp. baking powder
› 1/2 tsp. fine salt
› 2 1/2 cups (370 g) fresh blueberries
› 2 tsp. sugar (for topping)

Directions:

1. Blend the soy yogurt and sugar at low speed until smooth and frothy.
2. Mix the eggs one by one until well combined.
3. Sift the dry ingredients and alternate adding them with the soy milk.
4. Mash 1/2 cup of blueberries and stir by hand, then, by hand, mix the leftover blueberries.
5. Use vegetable oil to coat the muffin cups and the pan's surface. In a baking tray, put muffin cups.
6. Fill each muffin cup to the top with the mixture. Top muffins with sugar.
7. Preheat the oven to 375°F and bake for 25–30 minutes. Allow it cool for a minimum of 30 minutes in the pan before cautiously removing it.

NUTRITIONAL VALUES:

Sodium: 208 mg

Potassium: 119 mg

Phosphorus: 98 mg

Protein: 5 g

Carbs: 40 g

Fat: 9 g

THE CONFETTI OMELET

SERVINGS: 2

PREPARATION TIME: 20 minutes

Ingredients:

> 1 tsp. extra-virgin olive oil

> 1 tsp. canola oil

> 2 tbsp. diced red bell pepper

> 2 tbsp. diced orange bell pepper

> 2 tbsp. diced green onion

> 2 tbsp. chopped fresh mushrooms

> 1 tsp. minced garlic

> 2 medium eggs

> 2 medium egg whites

> 4 tbsp. unsweetened and unfortified soy milk

> 1/8 tsp. cumin powder

> 1/8 tsp. pepper powder

Directions:

1. Combine the olive and canola oil and sauté vegetables with garlic unless crisp-tender.

2. Lightly whisk the eggs, egg whites, and soy milk until smooth and creamy. Cumin and pepper should be added at this point.

3. Pour the egg mixture over the vegetables that have been sauteed.

4. Reduce the heat to low and cover for 1–2 minutes. Cover the omelet and raise the sides, allowing the raw egg to drip to the base of the pan.

5. Fold the omelet over in the pan after the egg is fully cooked.

6. Serve immediately after dividing the omelet into 2 pieces.

7. Garnish with a wedge of mushroom and green onion.

NUTRITIONAL VALUES:

Sodium: 186 mg

Potassium: 246 mg

Phosphorus:147 mg

Protein: 11 g

Carbs: 4 g

Fat: 1 g

NOURISHING EGG MUFFINS

SERVINGS: 8

PREPARATION TIME: 40 minutes

Ingredients:

› 1 cup (150 g) of yellow, red, and orange bell peppers
› 1 cup (125 g) onion
› 1/2-pound (225 g) pork, ground
› 1/4 tsp. poultry seasoning
› 1/4 tsp. garlic powder
› 1/4 tsp. powdered onion
› 1/2 tsp. Mrs. Dash® herb spice mix
› 8 medium eggs
› 2 tbsp. unsweetened and unfortified soy milk
› Pinch of fine salt

Directions:

1. Preheat the oven to 350ºF and coat a standard muffin pan with cooking spray.
2. Bell peppers and onion should be finely diced.
3. To prepare sausage, mix pork, poultry seasoning, garlic powder, onion powder, and Mrs. Dash spice mix in a mixing bowl.
4. Cook sausage crumbles in a non-stick pan until done; remove.
5. Combine the eggs, soy milk, and salt in a mixing bowl.
6. Combine the sausage shreds and vegetables in a mixing bowl.
7. Fill muffin pans halfway with the egg mixture, allowing room for the muffins to rise. Preheat the oven and bake for 18–22 minutes.

NUTRITIONAL VALUES:

Sodium: 154 mg

Potassium: 199 mg

Phosphorus: 153 mg

Protein: 11 g

Carbs: 4 g

Fat: 9 g

VANILLA PANCAKES WITH BERRY JAM

SERVINGS: 10 (1 = 2 pancakes)

PREPARATION TIME: 30 minutes

Ingredients:

> 2/3 cup (85 g) all-purpose flour
> 2 tbsp. sugar
> 4 medium eggs
> 1 cup (235 ml) unsweetened and unfortified soy milk
> 1/4 tsp. vanilla essence
> 2 tbsp. blueberry or berry jam

Directions:

1. Mix the flour and sugar in a medium mixing bowl. Using a whisk, thoroughly combine the eggs.

2. Combine the soy milk and vanilla essence in a mixing bowl. Blend until completely smooth.

3. Mix 3 tablespoons of the batter, coated with non-stick frying spray on a hot (8 x 10 inches) non-stick pan. To distribute the batter, gently rotate the pan. Cook until the bottom of the pancake is golden brown (approximately 45 seconds; ends will start to dry). Brown the opposite side of the pancake. Continue until you've used up all of the batter.

4. Serve small pancakes with fruit spread, folded or rolled. Fill with 1–2 tablespoons of blueberry or berry jam, if desired.

NUTRITIONAL VALUES:

Sodium: 38 mg

Potassium: 103 mg

Phosphorus: 79 mg

Protein: 5 g

Carbs: 37 g

Fat: 3 g

HOLIDAY BREAKFAST FRENCH TOAST

SERVINGS: 9

PREPARATION TIME: 1 hour 10 minutes

Ingredients:

> 3/4 cup (150 g) brown sugar

> 1/2 cup (120 ml) of extra-virgin olive oil

> 3 tsp. cinnamon powder

> 3 medium tart apples

> 1/2 cup (65 g) dried cranberries

> 6 medium eggs

> 1-pound (450 g) Italian bread

> 1 1/2 cup (350 ml) unsweetened and unenriched rice milk

> 3 tsp. vanilla

Directions:

1. Apples should be peeled, cored, and finely sliced or chopped.

2. Mix brown sugar, olive oil, and 1 teaspoon of cinnamon in a (13 x 9 inches) (33 x 23 cm) baking dish.

3. Cover the base of the baking tray with apples and cranberries.

4. Slice the bread into 3/4-inch (8-10 cm) pieces and place them on top of the apples.

5. Combine the eggs, rice milk, vanilla, and the leftover 2 teaspoons of cinnamon in a large mixing bowl. Pour the liquid over the bread and soak it thoroughly. Refrigerate for 4-24 hours after covering.

6. Preheat the oven to 375ºF.

7. Wrap in foil and bake for 30 minutes. Remove the lid and bake for 15 minutes, or until the top begins to brown.

8. Remove the dish from the oven and set it aside for 5 minutes before slicing it into 9 pieces.

9. Warm the dish before serving. While serving, dust the top with a pinch of icing sugar.

NUTRITIONAL VALUES:

Sodium: 380 mg

Potassium: 210 mg

Phosphorus: 136 mg

Protein: 9 g

Carbs: 63 g

Fat: 16 g

CHAPTER 4:
Scrumptious Snacks
& Appetizers Recipes

DELICIOUS ADDICTIVE PRETZELS

SERVINGS: 32 (1 = 1 oz.)

PREPARATION TIME: 1 hour

Ingredients:

> 1 (32 oz.) (900 g) bag pretzels, unsalted
> 1 cup (235 ml) canola oil
> 2 tbsp. Hidden Valley Ranch® seasoning mix
> 3 tsp. garlic powder
> 3 tsp. dill weed, dried

Directions:

1. Preheat the oven to 175ºF.
2. Pretzels should be spread out on 2 (18 x 13 inches) baking sheets so that they stay flat. Break large pretzels into chunks or use entire bite-size pretzels.
3. Combine the garlic powder and dill in a bowl. Half the seasonings should be set aside. Combine the dried seasoning mix plus 3/4 cup of canola oil with the other half. Drizzle equally over the pretzels, then coat with your hands to get an equal coating.
4. Cook the pretzels for 1 hour, turning them every 15 minutes.
5. Take the pretzels out of the oven and set them aside. Allow them to cool before tossing with the residual garlic powder, dill weed, and oil. Enjoy!

NUTRITIONAL VALUES:

Sodium: 60 mg

Potassium: 43 mg

Phosphorus: 28 mg

Protein: 2 g

Carbs: 22 g

Fat: 8 g

TOASTED PITA WITH ARTICHOKE RELISH

SERVINGS: 16 (1 = 2 tbsp. relish on 2 pita wedges)

PREPARATION TIME: 8 hours (Artichoke Relish), 8 minutes (Toasted Pita)

Ingredients:

> 14 oz. (400 g) artichoke hearts, canned

> 2 oz. (50 g) chopped pimento, canned

> 2 green onions

> 1 garlic clove

> 3 tbsp. grated or chopped tofu

> 2 tbsp. lemon juice

> 1 tbsp. extra-virgin olive oil

> 1/2 tsp. pepper powder

> 4 (7 inches) (18 cm) pita bread rounds

Directions:

1. Wash and dice the artichoke hearts and pimento. Chop the green onions finely and crush the garlic clove.

2. In a mixing bowl, add all ingredients, excluding the pitas, and stir thoroughly.

3. Refrigerate for 8 hours or overnight, covered.

4. Heat the oven to around 350ºF.

5. Divide the pita rounds by slicing them in half. Make 8 wedges by cutting each piece into quarters.

6. Put the pita wedges, flattened side down, on a baking tray, then coat with the cooking spray. Preheat the oven to 350ºF and bake for 8 minutes, or until gently browned.

7. Allow the pita wedges to cool completely before storing them in a sealed jar until ready to use.

8. With 1 tablespoon of artichoke relish, garnish each pita wedge.

NUTRITIONAL VALUES:

Sodium: 165 mg

Potassium: 102 mg

Phosphorus: 40 mg

Protein: 4 g

Carbs: 12 g

Fat: 3 g

SHRIMP AND VEGETABLE ROLLS

SERVINGS: 6 (1 = 2 rolls)

PREPARATION TIME: 30 minutes

Ingredients:

> 2 cups (85 g) Napa cabbage

> 1/2 cup (70 g) carrots

> 1/4 cup (35 g) green onions

> 2 tbsp. chopped cilantro

> 1 tsp. root ginger

> 1 ½ cup (250 g) raw shrimp

> 1 tbsp. hoisin sauce

> 1 tsp. brown sugar

> 1 tsp. powdered garlic

> 1/4 tsp. red chili flakes, (optional)

> 3 tbsp. water

> 12 (7 inches) (18 cm) square egg roll wrappers

Directions:

1. Preheat the oven to 400ºF. If the egg roll wrappers are frozen, set them out to defrost.

2. Cabbage and carrots should be finely diced. Slice the onions thinly; chop the cilantro, and grate the ginger root.

3. Wash and finely chop the shrimp.

4. In a hot non-stick pan, combine the cabbage, carrots, shrimp, and green onions.

5. Cook, turning periodically, over moderate flame until shrimp are pinkish and vegetables are transparent and tender (about 8 minutes).

6. Combine the chopped cilantro, hoisin sauce, brown sugar, powdered garlic, ginger, and red chili flakes in a large mixing bowl.

7. Mix well to ensure that the spices are equally distributed.

8. Cook for another 2 minutes, then turn off the heat and drain any extra liquid.

9. Grease a baking tray with the canola oil and put it aside while the vegetable shrimp mixture cools.

10. Put spring roll wrappers as follows on a work surface (or another sterile surface): Put one heaping spoonful of cooked mixture crosswise in each wrapper, approximately 1/3 of the way up from the top, but not directly in the middle. Fold two opposing wrapper sides over the mixture, then roll in the thin side first, then the extended side, until the roll is finished.

11. Put folded side down onto baking tray after dipping a finger in water and rubbing along the edge of the finished roll to seal it.

12. Spray canola oil on each packed spring roll.

13. Bake for 20 minutes, rotating after 10 minutes. The rolls should be gently toasted and crispy on the outside.

NUTRITIONAL VALUES:

Sodium: 291 mg

Potassium: 254 mg

Phosphorus: 165 mg

Protein: 15 g

Carbs: 31 g

Fat: 3 g

CRISPY BRUSSELS SPROUTS

SERVINGS: 2

PREPARATION TIME: 30 minutes

Ingredients:

> 15 brussels sprouts
> 1 tbsp. extra-virgin olive oil
> 1/4 tsp. pepper powder
> Pinch of fine salt

Directions:

1. Turn on the oven and preheat it to 400ºF.
2. Remove the outer leaves from the brussels sprouts to fill 4 cups. Don't throw away the inside, which for example you can use as a side dish for dinner.
3. Pour the leaves into a large enough bowl and mix with salt, oil, and ground pepper. At this point, slowly massage the leaves of the Brussels sprouts until they are evenly coated.
4. Take a large rimmed pan and spread the leaves in a single layer.
5. Roast the leaves for about 10 minutes, until they are crisp and golden at the right point.

NUTRITIONAL VALUES:

Sodium: 77mg

Potassium: 84 mg

Phosphorus: 15 mg

Protein: 0.8 g

Carbs: 2 g

Fat: 3.7 g

TILAPIA TAPAS WITH ADOBO CREAM

SERVINGS: 12 (1 = 4 wonton wraps)

PREPARATION TIME: 45 minutes

Ingredients:

> 6 (3 oz.) (85 g) pieces tilapia fillets

> 48 wonton wraps, small size

> 1 non-stick cooking spray

Adobo Sauce:

> 3 tbsp. Spanish paprika

> 1 tbsp. oregano

> 3 tbsp. ground coriander

> 1 tsp. black pepper

> 1 tsp. red pepper (flakes)

> 1/2 cup (120 ml) red wine vinegar

> 3 tbsp. extra-virgin olive oil

Coleslaw:

> 1/2 cup (110 g) mayonnaise

> 1 tbsp. fresh garlic (finely chopped)

> 1/4 cup (25 g) fresh green shallots (very thinly sliced)

> 1/4 cup (15 g) fresh coriander leaves (cut not too small)

> 4 cups (360 g) cabbage, finely chopped

> 1/4 cup (60 ml) fresh lemon juice

Directions:

1. Turn on and heat the oven to 400ºF.
2. Combine and mix all the adobo ingredients well and leave them aside for the next steps.
3. Leave the tilapia fillets to marinate for about 30 minutes in 1/2 cup of adobo sauce.
4. Grease the pan with a little extra-virgin olive oil and cook the fish for about 7-8 minutes at 200ºF. At this point, turn the fish to the other side and cook for another 7-8 minutes.
5. Once cooked, set the fish aside.
6. At this point, combine and mix well the un-used adobo sauce, garlic, mayonnaise, coriander, and shallot in a bowl of sufficient size.
7. Then, add the cabbage and mix slowly to cover it completely.
8. Use cooking spray on a miniature muffin pan.
9. Use wonton wrappers to line muffin cups.
10. Bake the wontons for about 5 minutes at 180ºF, and once cooled, remove them from the pan.
11. Chop the fish into 48 equal parts and place on the wontons, garnish them with equal amounts of coleslaw and serve with a few coriander leaves.

NUTRITIONAL VALUES:

Sodium: 271 mg

Potassium: 267 mg

Phosphorus: 115 mg

Protein: 12 g

Carbs: 23 g

Fat: 12 g

LOW SODIUM BUFFALO WINGS

SERVINGS: 12 (1 = 2 wings)

PREPARATION TIME: 1 hour 20 minutes

Ingredients:

> 1/3 cup (75 g) Tabasco® hot pepper sauce
> 1/4 cup (55 g) red pepper sauce (roasted)
> 1/4 cup (55 g) tomato sauce (low sodium)
> 9 tbsp. extra-virgin olive oil
> 1/2 tsp. garlic powder
> 1/2 tsp. Italian seasoning mix (dry)
> 24 chicken wing drumettes

Directions:

1. Heat the oven to around 400ºF.
2. In a skillet, stir to mix the hot sauce, red pepper and tomato sauce, extra-virgin olive oil, garlic powder, as well as Italian spices. Turn off the heat in the pan.
3. In a baking dish, add the chicken wings.
4. Bake about 30-35 minutes after pouring the sauce onto the wings.
5. Serve the wings immediately, or keep them warm in a covered skillet or crock pot unless ready to eat.

NUTRITIONAL VALUES:

Sodium: 64 mg

Potassium: 105 mg

Phosphorus: 61 mg

Protein: 8 g

Carbs: 0 g

Fat: 11 g

STRAWBERRY AND BLUEBERRY TOFU SMOOTHIE

SERVINGS: 2

PREPARATION TIME: 16 minutes

Ingredients:

> 1-pound (450 g) fresh strawberries
> 2 cups (295 g) blueberries
> 9 oz. (255 g) silken tofu
> 1/2 tsp. powdered ginger
> 1 tsp. vanilla extract
> 1/4 tsp. rum extract
> 1 tbsp. honey
> 1 tsp. lemon juice

Directions:

1. Clean and peel the strawberries.
2. Blend all the ingredients at high speed until a creamy consistency is obtained and serve immediately.

NUTRITIONAL VALUES:

Sodium: 25 mg

Potassium: 364 mg

Phosphorus: 94 mg

Protein: 5 g

Carbs: 25 g

Fat: 3 g

GRILLED MEATBALLS

SERVINGS: 24 (1 = 2 meatballs)

PREPARATION TIME: 1 hour 20 min

Ingredients:

> 1/2 cup (60 g) onion
> 3 pounds (1.360 kg) ground beef
> 2 medium eggs
> 1/2 cup (120 ml) unsweetened and unen-riched rice milk
> 1 cup (80 g) raw oatmeal
> 1 tbsp. thyme, dry
> 1 tsp. oregano, dry
> 1/2 tsp. pepper powder
> 1 cup (280 g) barbecue sauce
> 1/3 cup (80 ml) water

Directions:

1. Preheat the oven to 375ºF.
2. Dice the onion and whisk eggs.
3. In a large mixing bowl, add all ingredients (excluding barbecue sauce and water) and stir to combine.
4. Put on a baking sheet, then roll into (1 inch) balls.
5. Cook about 10-15 minutes, or until meatballs are well cooked.
6. In a heating dish or a Crock pot® set on medium, combine the barbecue sauce and water. Stir in the meatballs. Cover and set aside unless ready to serve.

NUTRITIONAL VALUES:

Sodium: 179 mg

Potassium: 207 mg

Phosphorus: 106 mg

Protein: 11 g

Carbs: 6 g

Fat: 12 g

CHICKEN NUGGETS AND SWEET MUSTARD SAUCE

SERVINGS: 12 (1 = 3 nuggets with 1 tbsp. sauce)

PREPARATION TIME: 51 minutes

Ingredients:

> 1 tbsp. mustard, yellow

> 1/2 cup (110 g) mayonnaise

> 1/3 cup (110 g) honey

> 2 tsp. Worcestershire sauce

> 1 large egg

> 2 tbsp. unsweetened and unfortified soy milk

> 3 cups (80 g) cornflakes

> 1-pound (450 g) boneless chicken breast

Directions:

1. In a medium bowl, combine the mustard, mayonnaise, honey, and Worcestershire sauce. Chill the sauce unless the nuggets are done, then use them as a condiment.

2. Preheat the oven to 400ºF.

3. Chicken breast should be cut into 36 bite-sized chunks.

4. Crush the cornflakes and pour them into a big zip-lock bag.

5. In a medium bowl, whisk together the beaten egg and soy milk. After dipping the chicken pieces in the mixture of eggs, shake them in a zip-lock bag to cover them with cornflakes crumbs.

6. Bake nuggets for about 15 minutes or unless done on a baking tray coated with non-stick baking spray.

NUTRITIONAL VALUES:

Sodium: 156 mg

Potassium: 98 mg

Phosphorus: 69 mg

Protein: 9 g

Carbs: 14 g

Fat: 8 g

CUCUMBER SPREAD CREAM

Ingredients:

> 8 oz. (225 g) soy cream (like silken tofu)
> 1 cucumber
> 1 tsp. onion
> 1 tbsp. mayonnaise

Directions:

1. Set out the soy cream to soften.
2. Set aside cucumbers that have been peeled, seeded, and coarsely minced. Chop the onion finely.
3. In a small mixing bowl, combine soy cream, onion, and mayonnaise and mix thoroughly.
4. Toss the cucumber into the mixture until it is equally distributed.

NUTRITIONAL VALUES:

Sodium: 99 mg

Potassium: 72 mg

Phosphorus: 35 mg

Protein: 3 g

Carbs: 3 g

Fat: 9 g

STUFFED DEVILED EGGS

SERVINGS: 2 (1 = 2 egg halves)

PREPARATION TIME: 30 minutes

Ingredients:

> 2 eggs
> 2 tsp. canned pimento
> 2 tsp. dried mustard
> 2 tbsp. mayonnaise
> 1/2 tsp. ground black pepper
> 1/8 tsp. paprika

Directions:

1. Boil the eggs for a long time. Drain and let them cool.
2. Scrape the eggs, then cut them lengthwise to remove the yolk.
3. Combine pimento, yolk, dried mustard, mayonnaise, and black pepper in a mixing bowl.
4. Fill egg whites with equal portions of the mixture.
5. Paprika should be sprinkled over the eggs.

NUTRITIONAL VALUES:

Sodium: 175 mg

Potassium: 65 mg

Phosphorus: 93 mg

Protein: 7 g

Carbs: 2 g

Fat: 10 g

HEALTHY BAKED FALAFEL

SERVINGS: 8 (1 = 3 falafel)

PREPARATION TIME: 50 minutes

Ingredients:

> 1-pound (450 g) chickpeas, dry
> 2 green onions
> 1/2 cup (30 g) parsley
> 2 cups (105 g) white onion
> 4 garlic cloves
> 1/4 cup (60 ml) lemon juice
> 1 ½ cup (180 g) flour
> 3/4 tsp. fine salt
> 1 tsp. coriander, minced
> 1 tbsp. cumin powder
> 1/4 tsp. black pepper
> 1/4 tsp. cayenne pepper

Directions:

1. In a large saucepan, cover chickpeas with water and soak for 24 hours at room temperature.

2. Slice the white onion, green onions, parsley, and garlic thoroughly.

3. Chickpeas should be drained and rinsed. Combine the green and white onion, minced parsley, chopped garlic, juice of lemon, flour, salt, minced coriander, cumin powder, black pepper, and cayenne pepper in a stick blender.

4. Pulse until the mixture resembles a coarse meal or paste. (Be careful not to over-process). Based on the size of the food processor, you might need to do this in two batches. Remove any big chunks of chickpeas and mix everything with a fork.

5. Allow 2 hours for the falafel mixture to chill.

6. Preheat the oven to 400ºF.

7. Using cooking spray, coat a muffin pan.

8. Make 24 balls using a scoop or by rolling the mixture into balls and placing them directly in the muffin tray. Preheat the oven to 350°F and cook for 7 minutes. Take out the falafel from the oven, flip it over, and bake for another 7 minutes.

NUTRITIONAL VALUES:

Sodium: 238 mg

Potassium: 547 mg

Phosphorus: 169 mg

Protein: 13 g

Carbs: 43 g

Fat: 6 g

CHAPTER 5:

Flavorful Lunch Recipes

ASIAN ORANGE CHICKEN

SERVINGS: 4

PREPARATION TIME: 3 hours 20 minutes

Ingredients:

> 1 ¾ cup (410 ml) water
> 2 tbsp. orange juice
> 1/4 cup (60 ml) lemon juice
> 1/3 cup (80 ml) rice vinegar, unseasoned
> 2 tbsp. soy sauce (low sodium)
> 1 tbsp. zest orange
> 1/3 cup (65 g) brown sugar, packed

> 1/2 tsp. fresh ginger root
> 1 garlic clove
> 2 tbsp. green onion
> 1/4 tsp. red pepper flakes
> 1/2-pound (225 g) chicken breasts, boneless and skinless
> 2 ½ tbsp. cornstarch
> 3 tbsp. extra-virgin olive oil

Directions:

1. Mince the garlic and ginger root. Then, chop the green onion.

2. Set a pot over medium-high heat with 1 ½ cup (355 ml) of water, orange juice, lemon juice, rice vinegar, and soy sauce. Combine the zest of orange, brown sugar, chopped ginger, chopped garlic, diced onion, and red pepper flakes in a large mixing bowl. Bring the water to a boil. Remove from the heat and set aside to cool for 10-15 minutes.

3. Place the chicken in a Ziploc bag and cut it into 1/2-inch (1,27 cm) pieces. Transfer 1 cup of sauce into the bag after the contents of the pot have cooled. Save the rest of the sauce. Refrigerate for a minimum of 2 hours after sealing the bag.

4. In a medium saucepan, heat the oil over moderate flame. In the same skillet, sear the marinated chicken on each side. Strain on a paper towel-lined dish and put it aside.

5. Remove the pan from the heat and incorporate the sauce. Over moderate flame, bring to a boil. Combine the cornstarch as well as the leftover 1/4 cup of water in a mixing bowl; whisk into the sauce. Lower the heat, add the chicken chunks and cook, stirring periodically, for approximately 5 minutes.

6. Serve warm, divided into 4 pieces.

NUTRITIONAL VALUES:

Sodium: 339 mg

Potassium: 239 mg

Phosphorus: 117 mg

Protein: 14 g

Carbs: 19 g

Fat: 12 g

ASIAN STYLE TURKEY AND RICE

Ingredients:

> 1 cup (220 g) un-cooked rice
> 1 onion
> 1 red bell pepper
> 2 celery stalks
> 3 garlic cloves
> 1 tbsp. grated ginger
> 1 tbsp. extra-virgin olive oil
> 1 pound (450 g) ground turkey
> 1 tbsp. Mrs. Dash garlic and herb spice mix
> 8 oz. (225 g) broccoli florets, refrigerated
> 1/2 cup (115 ml) chicken stock (low sodium)
> 2 tbsp. brown sugar
> 1 ½ tbsp. coconut aminos
> 1 teaspoon chili sauce (Sriracha)
> 2 tbsp. chopped cilantro

Directions:

1. Cook the rice as per the package directions. Allow frozen broccoli to defrost. Chop the onion, celery, and garlic cloves; shred the ginger, and cut the cilantro.

2. In a wide non-stick pan, sprinkle extra-virgin olive oil and cook over medium flame. Brown the turkey in the pan. Mix the Mrs. Dash herb spice halfway during cooking. Remove the turkey from the pan after it has finished cooking.

3. Cook for 5 minutes over a moderate flame with the onion, peppers, and celery in the same pan. Cook for another 3 minutes after adding the garlic and ginger.

4. When the vegetables are tender, toss in the frozen broccoli and cook for a few minutes longer.

5. In a small mixing dish, add stock, brown sugar, coconut aminos, and Sriracha sauce.

6. Return the cooked turkey to the pan and whisk in the sauce to incorporate.

7. In a bowl, combine 1/2 cup rice, turkey, and vegetable combination. If desired, garnish with chopped cilantro. Enjoy!

NUTRITIONAL VALUES:

Sodium: 261 mg

Potassium: 649 mg

Phosphorus: 320 mg

Protein: 26 g

Carbs: 42 g

Fat: 14 g

BAKED CHICKEN SALAD

SERVINGS: 6

PREPARATION TIME: 50 minutes

Ingredients:

> 12 oz. (350 g) uncooked boneless and skin-less chicken breast
> 1/2 cup (100 g) diced celery
> 1/4 cup (60 g) diced onion
> 1/2 cup (50 g) diced canned mushrooms
> 1/4 cup (60 g) diced canned water chest-nuts
> 1/2 cup (115 g) mayonnaise
> 1/2 cup (120 g) of soy cream
> 2 tbsp. lemon juice, freshly squeezed
> 1/2 tsp. Tabasco® sauce
> 1 cup (60 g) crumbled chow mein noodles

Directions:

1. Boil the chicken breasts until they are fully done. Drain.
2. Cut the chicken into chunks. To use it in the recipe, weigh 2 cups.
3. Drain and rinse the mushrooms well.
4. Add all ingredients to a bowl and mix, except the chow mein noodles. Mix thoroughly.
5. Put a (9 x 9 inches) (23 x 23 cm) baking sheet greased with extra-virgin olive oil tray halfway with the mixture. On top, distribute noodles.
6. Preheat the oven to 350°F and bake for 30 minutes.
7. Serve by slicing into 6 equal pieces.

NUTRITIONAL VALUES:

Sodium: 283 mg

Potassium: 192 mg

Phosphorus: 117 mg

Protein: 16 g

Carbs: 9 g

Fat: 22 g

CHICKEN VEGETABLE LINGUINE

SERVINGS: 6

PREPARATION TIME: 40 minutes

Ingredients:

> 1 pound (450 g) chicken breasts, boneless and skinless
> 3 tbsp. extra-virgin olive oil
> 4 oz. (115 g) uncooked whole-wheat linguine
> 3/4 cup (55 g) broccoli florets
> 3/4 cup (55 g) florets cauliflower
> 3/4 cup (90 g) baby carrots
> 16 grape tomatoes
> 2 tbsp. lemon juice
> 3/4 tsp. Mrs. Dash® herb spice mix

Directions:

1. Cut the chicken into tiny strips.
2. On moderate flame, heat 2 tablespoons of extra-virgin olive oil in a skillet.
3. Cook until the chicken is done in the pan.
4. As per the package instructions, cook 4 pounds of linguine.
5. Broccoli and cauliflower should be cut into bite-size pieces.
6. When the chicken is done, add broccoli, cauliflower, carrots, tomatoes, and lemon juice. Simmer for 3 minutes, covered.
7. Bring the strained pasta to the pan, then whisk 1 tablespoon of extra-virgin olive oil.
8. Mix Mrs. Dash and cook on medium for 5 minutes.

NUTRITIONAL VALUES:

Sodium: 58 mg

Potassium: 559 mg

Phosphorus: 287 mg

Protein: 23 g

Carbs: 32 g

Fat: 9 g

COUSCOUS WITH VEGETABLES

SERVINGS: 5

PREPARATION TIME: 30 minutes

Ingredients:

> 1 tbsp. extra-virgin olive oil
> 1/2 cup (70 g) peas, refrigerated
> 1/4 cup (25 g) raw mushrooms
> 1/2 cup (65 g) onion
> 1 garlic clove
> 2 tbsp. white wine (dry)
> 1/2 tsp. basil leaves, dried
> 1/8 tsp. black pepper
> 2 tbsp. fresh parsley
> 1/2 cup (90 g) raw couscous

Directions:

1. Place frozen peas outside to defrost. Chop the onion and mushrooms thinly; then, mince the garlic. Finely chopped the parsley.
2. Heat extra-virgin olive oil in a non-stick skillet.
3. At this point, add peas, onion, mushrooms, garlic, and wine. Cook for 5 minutes, stirring frequently.
4. Blend the spices well. Stir in the parsley. Remove the pan from the heat and put it aside.
5. Follow the package instructions for couscous preparation.
6. Toss the vegetable mixture with the couscous in a large mixing bowl. Serve right away.

NUTRITIONAL VALUES:

Sodium: 32 mg

Potassium: 99 mg

Phosphorus: 51 mg

Protein: 3 g

Carbs: 18 g

Fat: 2 g

CHALLAH HOLIDAY DRESSING

SERVINGS: 16

PREPARATION TIME: 1 hour 30 minutes

Ingredients:

> 2 pounds (900 g) Challah bread
> 2 onions
> 4 stalks celery
> 2 large green bell peppers
> 2 large carrots
> 4 garlic cloves
> 5 tbsp. of extra virgin olive oil
> 2 tbsp. poultry seasoning
> 1 pound (450 g) ground turkey
> 2 cups (480 g) turkey broth (low sodium)
> 3 medium eggs
> 1/2 cup (30 g) fresh parsley

Directions:

1. Let challah loaves remain overnight after dividing them into pieces.
2. Preheat the oven to 350ºF. Dice the onion, celery, green peppers, carrots, and parsley. Garlic should be minced.
3. Pour 4 tablespoons of olive oil in a large skillet over medium heat.
4. Cook until the ground turkey is browned. Take the turkey out of the pan and put it aside to cool.
5. In the same pan, saute the onion, celery, green peppers, and carrots until soft. Heat for a further 1-2 minutes after adding the garlic.
6. With the leftover tablespoon of olive oil, prepare an oven-safe pan. Cover the bread pieces with poultry spice and place them in the pan.
7. Beat the eggs and fold them into the chilled turkey mixture.
8. Toss the bread with the egg and turkey combination, as well as 1/4 cup of minced parsley. Mix gently.
9. Mix the turkey broth until everything is well combined. The mixture will seem mushy.
10. Bake for approximately 40 minutes with the pan covered. Remove the top and bake for another 20 minutes.
11. While serving, top with the extra parsley.

NUTRITIONAL VALUES:

Sodium: 279 mg

Potassium: 265 mg

Phosphorus: 155 mg

Protein: 13 g

Carbs: 31 g

Fat: 10 g

CEVICHE CARIBE

Ingredients:

- › 12 large peeled, chilled and cooked shrimp
- › 2 green onions
- › 1 large tomato
- › 1 banana pepper, medium yellow
- › 1 chili pepper, fresh and hot
- › 2 tbsp. cilantro, chopped
- › 3 tbsp. lime juice
- › 2 tbsp. white distilled vinegar
- › 1 tsp. powdered garlic
- › 1 cup (170 g) fresh pineapple
- › 1 tbsp. extra-virgin olive oil

Directions:

1. Remove the tails from the shrimp and thaw them. Chop the vegetables into bite-sized chunks.

2. Combine green onions, tomato, peppers, and cilantro in a food processor, then pulse on-off to mince to a very fine consistency. The texture should be chunky. Toss the lime juice, vinegar, and garlic powder.

3. Add the diced shrimp and olive oil to the mix in a serving dish.

4. Fresh pineapple should be peeled and cored. Put in a food blender and pulse until coarsely chopped. Combine the pineapple, shrimp, and vegetables. Integrate the ingredients into a mixing bowl.

5. Before serving, chill for at least 30 minutes.

NUTRITIONAL VALUES:

Sodium: 114 mg

Potassium: 145 mg

Phosphorus: 42 mg

Protein: 4 g

Carbs: 5 g

Fat: 3 g

CHICKEN AND SUMMER SQUASH BOW-TIE PASTA

SERVINGS: 4

PREPARATION TIME: 40 minutes

Ingredients:

> 6 oz. uncooked whole-wheat pasta, bow-tie

> 3 tbsp. extra-virgin olive oil

> 8 oz. chicken breasts, boneless and skinless

> 2 cups (226 g) summer squash, refrigerated

> 1 tsp. Mrs. Dash® table mix seasoning

> 1/8 tsp. fine salt

> 2 tbsp. grated extra-firm tofu

Directions:

1. Dice the chicken and save it for later.

2. Prepare bow-tie pasta according to package directions, omitting the salt. Drain.

3. In a skillet over medium heat, place 2 tablespoons of olive oil and the diced chicken, cooking until it is no longer pink inside.

4. Frozen squash should be added to the pan with the chicken. Bring to a simmer.

5. Season the chicken and squash with Mrs. Dash's table mix seasoning and salt.

6. In a sufficiently large bowl, combine the cooked pasta with the chicken mixture and 1 tablespoon of olive oil.

7. Before serving, divide the mixture into 4 pieces and top each with 1/2 tablespoon of shredded extra-firm tofu.

NUTRITIONAL VALUES:

Sodium: 115 mg

Potassium: 296 mg

Phosphorus: 156 mg

Protein: 19 g

Carbs: 32 g

Fat: 10 g

CHICKEN ENCHILADAS

SERVINGS: 6 (1 = 1/4 cup)

PREPARATION TIME: 1 hour

Ingredients:

> 2 tbsp. canola oil
> 12 (6 inches) (15 cm) corn tortillas
> 3 cups (420 g) cooked, shredded chicken breast
> 2/3 cup (60 g) coarsely chopped green on-ion
> 1/2 cup (132 g) of soy cream
> 1 cup (260 g) enchilada sauce

Directions:

1. Preheat the oven to 375ºF.
2. In a saucepan, heat the oil.
3. Gently cook each tortilla by dipping it into the pan and then removing it to a dish.
4. Add 1/4 cup of shredded chicken, 1 table-spoon of onion, and 2 teaspoons of soy cream in the middle of each tortilla.
5. Roll up every single enchilada and put it in a baking tray.
6. Top with 1 ½ cup of enchilada sauce.
7. Heat the baking tray in the oven for about 20-30 minutes, or until done.

NUTRITIONAL VALUES:

Sodium: 169 mg

Potassium: 450 mg

Phosphorus: 331 mg

Protein: 23 g

Carbs: 29 g

Fat: 14 g

BARLEY AND BEEF STEW

SERVINGS: 6

PREPARATION TIME: 1 hour 20 minutes

Ingredients:

> 1 cup (200 g) raw pearl barley
> 1 pound (450 g) stew meat (lean beef)
> 2 tbsp. white all-purpose flour
> 1/4 tsp. black pepper
> 1/2 tsp. salt
> 2 tbsp. canola oil
> 1/2 cup (70 g) onion
> 1 celery stalk, large
> 1 garlic clove
> 2 carrots
> 2 bay leaves
> 1 tsp. Mrs. Dash® herb seasoning

Directions:

1. Steep barley for approximately 1 hour in 2 cups of water.

2. Dice the onion and celery. Mince the garlic. Slice the carrots 1/4-inch thick. Cut the beef into 1-1/2-inch pieces.

3. In a plastic bag, combine flour, black pepper, and stew meat. Dust the stew meat using flour by twisting it.

4. Cook the stew meat in a large 4-quart saucepan with oil. Take the meat out of the pot.

5. In the meat drippings, saute and mix onion, celery, and garlic for 2 minutes. Bring 2 cups of water to a boil in a separate pan. Put the meat back in the pot. Season with salt and bay leaves. Reduce the heat to a low simmer.

6. Drain and rinse the barley before adding it to the saucepan. Saute for 1 hour with the lid on. Every 15 minutes, give it a little stir.

7. Add diced carrots and Mrs. Dash® herb spice after 1 hour. Continue cooking for another hour. If necessary, add more water to avoid sticking.

NUTRITIONAL VALUES:

Sodium: 221 mg

Potassium: 368 mg

Phosphorus: 174 mg

Protein: 21 g

Carbs: 21 g

Fat: 8 g

CHICKEN VERONIQUE

SERVINGS: 2

PREPARATION TIME: 30 minutes

Ingredients:

> 2 (4 ounces each) skinless and boneless chicken breasts
> 2 tbsp. of extra-virgin olive oil
> 1/2 shallot
> 1 tsp. cornstarch
> 2 tbsp. white wine, dry
> 2 tbsp. chicken stock (low sodium)
> 1/2 cup (75 g) green grapes, seedless
> 1 tsp. tarragon (dry)
> 1/4 cup (65 g) of soy cream

Directions:

1. Warm the olive oil in an (8 inches) pan and cook the chicken breasts on each side unless lightly browned. Transfer to a plate.

2. Dice the shallot finely, then saute until translucent.

3. In a small mixing bowl, combine the cornstarch, wine, and stock. Pour into the saucepan, stirring constantly, and then incorporate the chicken breasts. Saute for 5-6 minutes, covered.

4. While the chicken is cooking, slice the grapes in halves.

5. Cover the pan with a lid to hold the chicken warm. Bring the cream and tarragon to a simmer in a saucepan. Saute until the grapes are cooked thoroughly in the sauce.

6. Place one chicken breast on a dish, then garnish with sauce and grapes.

NUTRITIONAL VALUES:

Sodium: 166 mg

Potassium: 542 mg

Phosphorus: 291 mg

Protein: 26 g

Carbs: 9 g

Fat: 17 g

CABBAGE BORSCH

SERVINGS: 12

PREPARATION TIME: 2 hrs.

Ingredients:

> 2 pounds (900 g) beef steaks

> 6 cups (1420 ml) ice water

> 2 tbsp. extra-virgin olive oil

> 1/2 cup (120 g) tomato sauce (low sodium)

> 1 cabbage

> 1 cup (130 g) onion

> 1 cup (140 g) carrots

> 1 cup (130 g) turnips

> 3/4 tsp. fine salt

> 1 tsp. pepper

> 6 tbsp. lemon juice

> 4 tbsp. sugar

NUTRITIONAL VALUES:

Sodium: 241 mg

Potassium: 387 mg

Phosphorus: 159 mg

Protein: 18 g

Carbs: 10 g

Fat: 9 g

Directions:

1. In a large saucepan, place the steak. Fill the saucepan with enough water to fully cover the meat. Bring to a simmer, covered with a lid. Lower the heat to a gentle simmer and cook until the meat is done and easily shreds.

2. Take the meat out of the saucepan and shred it with the help of a fork.

3. Cut the cabbage into small pieces.

4. Onions, carrots, and turnips should all be peeled and diced.

5. Remove the water from the saucepan and stir in the extra-virgin olive oil, tomato sauce, diced cabbage, diced onion, carrots, turnips, and shredded meat.

6. Incorporate salt and pepper to taste, lemon juice, and sugar.

7. Cook for 1 or 1 ½ hour on low flame, or until all vegetables are tender. If preferred, season with additional lemon and pepper before serving.

CHAPTER 6:
Flavorsome Dinner Recipes

ALL AMERICAN MEATLOAF

SERVINGS: 6

PREPARATION TIME: 50 minutes

Ingredients:

> 2 tbsp. onion
> 20 squares saltine crackers (tops unsalted)
> 1 pound (450 g) ground beef (lean)
> 1 large egg
> 2 tbsp. unsweetened soy milk
> 1/4 tsp. black pepper
> 1/3 cup (75 g) catsup
> 1 tbsp. brown sugar
> 1/2 tsp. apple cider vinegar
> 1 tsp. water

Directions:

1. Preheat the oven to 350ºF.
2. Chop the onion finely. Smash crackers using a rolling pin in a wide zip-top bag.
3. Using non-stick cooking spray, cover a loaf pan.
4. Combine smashed crackers, chopped onion, ground beef, egg, soy milk, and black pepper in a large mixing bowl. Mix thoroughly.
5. Fill a loaf pan halfway with the mixture. Bake for about 40 minutes.
6. In a separate bowl, combine catsup, brown sugar, vinegar, and water to prepare the topping.
7. Remove the cooked meatloaf from the oven and pour the sauce over it.
8. Return the pan to the oven and bake for another 10 minutes, or until the internal temperature hits 160ºF.
9. Serve by slicing into 6 pieces.

NUTRITIONAL VALUES:

Sodium: 297 mg

Potassium: 254 mg

Phosphorus: 146 mg

Protein: 17 g

Carbs: 14 g

Fat: 9 g

QUINOA WITH SEARED SCALLOPS

SERVINGS: 3

PREPARATION TIME: 30-35 minutes

Ingredients:

> 2 tbsp. extra-virgin olive oil
> 3 sliced scallions (divide the green part from the white part)
> 1 cup (185 g) quinoa
> 1 cup (250 ml) water
> 2 blood oranges
> 3 tbsp. toasted sliced almonds (divided)
> ¼ cup (60 g) fresh cilantro (chopped)
> 1 tsp. cumin powder
> ½ tsp. ground coriander, divided
> ¼ tsp. fine salt
> ½ pound (230 g) dried scallops

Directions:

1. Heat 1 tablespoon of extra-virgin olive oil in a saucepan over medium heat.
2. At this point, cook the whites of the shallots and continue stirring, for about 60 seconds, until they are golden brown.
3. Put the quinoa in the saucepan as well, continuing to stir for another 60 seconds until it becomes toasted too. Then, add the water, and once it comes to a boil, lower the heat and cover, letting it cook over low heat.
4. After about 13-14 minutes, turn off the heat and, always leaving the pot covered, let it rest for 5-6 minutes.
5. During this time, prepare the oranges, using a sharp knife to remove the peel, the white part, and the outer membrane of the cloves, trying to leave the pulp intact.
6. Take a large enough bowl and gently mix the shallot, coriander, 1/2 teaspoon of cumin, 1/4 teaspoon of coriander powder, and a little salt.
7. Dry the scallops and then sprinkle them using the remaining 1/4 teaspoon of coriander and 1/2 teaspoon of cumin.
8. Take a non-stick (or cast iron) pan and put the remaining 1 tablespoon of olive oil by heating it over medium heat. At this point, cook the scallops for 2-3 minutes per side, until they are golden in color.
9. Take a bowl, slowly mix the quinoa with the orange wedges, and finally add the scallops and almonds on top.

Advice: It is important to buy "dried" sea scallops. "Wet" scallops are treated with sodium tripolyphosphate (STP), are richer in salt, have a different texture, and do not brown properly.

NUTRITIONAL VALUES:

Sodium: 587 mg

Potassium: 375 mg

Phosphorus: 513 mg

Protein: 20 g

Carbs: 39 g

Fat: 13 g

TUNA AND SESAME SALAD

SERVINGS: 4

PREPARATION TIME: 25-30 minutes

Ingredients:

> ¼ lemon juice
> 3 tbsp. canola oil
> 2 tbsp. low sodium soy sauce
> 1 tbsp. toasted sesame oil
> 1 ½ tsp. sugar
> 1 ½ tsp. fresh ginger (chopped)
> 2 (5 ounces) (140 g) cans tuna (drained)
> 1 cup (140 g) peas
> 2 shallots (sliced)
> 6 cups (90 g) cabbage or romaine lettuce (thinly sliced)
> 4 radishes (sliced)
> ¼ cup (5 g) fresh coriander leaves
> 1 tbsp. sesame seeds
> Pinch freshly ground pepper

Directions:

1. Toasted sesame oil turns a food like canned tuna into an elegant dinner. Let's begin!
2. Whisk the lemon juice, canola and sesame oil, sugar, soy sauce, and ginger in a small bowl.
3. Combine 3 tablespoons of the dressing with tuna, peas, and scallions in a medium bowl.
4. Break the cabbage into 4 plates. Place about 1/2 cup of the tuna mixture in the center of each plate and garnish with radishes, cilantro, and sesame seeds. Season with the remaining seasoning and pepper.

NUTRITIONAL VALUES:

Sodium: 367 mg

Potassium: 161 mg

Phosphorus: 130 mg

Protein: 10 g

Carbs: 9 g

Fat: 15 g

GRILLED SALMON SANDWICH WITH CHIPOTLE MAYONNAISE

SERVINGS: 4

PREPARATION TIME: 25-30 minutes

Ingredients:

> 1 tbsp. extra-virgin olive oil
> 1 tbsp. lime juice
> 1/2 tsp. seasoning (lemon-pepper)
> 8 oz. (220 g) (2 each) salmon fillets
> 1/4 cup (55 g) chipotle mayonnaise
> 4 sourdough bread slices
> 1 cup (20 g) arugula
> 1/2 cup (75 g) roasted red peppers, chopped

Directions:

1. Heat the grill to moderate. Coat fillets of salmon with 1 tablespoon of extra-virgin olive oil. Cover the fillets on the grill. Cook for 10-15 minutes, or until the flesh readily flakes.

2. Combine the residual olive oil, lime juice, and lemon-pepper spice mix in a small bowl.

3. Drizzle the sourdough bread with extra-virgin olive oil and put on the grill grates, grilling for 1-2 minutes on each side, or unless toasted, while the salmon is cooling.

4. Remove the salmon from the grill and set it aside to rest for 5-10 minutes, wrapped in foil on a dish. Strip the skin.

5. While the salmon is cooling, toast the sourdough bread on the grill grates for 1-2 minutes on each side.

6. To make the outward-facing sandwich, begin with sourdough bread and an even layer of chipotle mayo, followed by the arugula, salmon, and roasted red peppers.

NUTRITIONAL VALUES:

Sodium: 334 mg

Potassium: 320 mg

Phosphorus: 134 mg

Protein: 13 g

Carbs: 20 g

Fat: 12 g

RICE WITH VEGETABLES AND CRISPY TOFU

SERVINGS: 4

PREPARATION TIME: 25-30 minutes

Ingredients:

> 16 oz. (450 g) tofu (extra firm)
> 1/2 red bell pepper, chopped
> 1 garlic clove
> 1 ½ tbsp. low-sodium soy sauce
> 1 ½ tbsp. lime juice
> 2 tsp. sugar
> 2 tbsp. cornstarch
> 2 egg whites
> 1/2 cup (45 g) breadcrumbs, unseasoned
> 1 ½ tbsp. canola oil
> 1 tbsp. extra-virgin olive oil
> 1 cup (80 g) florets, fresh broccoli
> 1 tsp. Mrs. Dash® herb spice mix
> 1/8 tsp. ground black pepper
> 1/8 tsp. cayenne pepper
> 1/2 tsp. sesame seeds
> 2 cups (315 g) white steamed rice

NUTRITIONAL VALUES:

Sodium: 583 mg

Potassium: 316 mg

Phosphorus: 176 mg

Protein: 18 g

Carbs: 46 g

Fat: 15 g

Directions:

1. To prepare the tofu, cut it into cubes. Bell pepper should be cut into strips, and the garlic clove should be chopped.

2. In a medium bowl, combine low-sodium soy sauce, lime juice, and sugar. Place aside.

3. Combine cornstarch, egg whites, plus breadcrumbs in 3 different bowls. To prepare the tofu cubes, first coat them in cornstarch, next egg whites, and finally bread crumbs.

4. In a pan or wok, heat canola oil and stir-fried covered tofu till golden brown and crispy. Take the tofu out of the pan and put it aside.

5. Melt the sesame oil in the same saucepan. Broccoli and red bell pepper ribbons should be stir-fried till crisp-tender. Cook for 1 minute after adding the minced garlic, Mrs. Dash spice mix, black pepper, and cayenne pepper.

6. Return the tofu to the pan and mix with the vegetables. Pour the soy-lime juice concoction over the top, then toss the sesame seeds. Remove from the heat and split into 4 equal portions. With 1/2 cup of rice, serve.

PORK CHOPS AND PEACHES

Ingredients:

> 1/2 cup (60 g) all-purpose flour
> 1 medium egg
> 1 cup (235 ml) water
> 3/4 cup cornflake crumbs
> 6 (21 oz.) (600 g) pork chops (center-cut)
> 2 tbsp. extra-virgin olive oil
> 1 tsp. paprika
> 1/4 tsp. fine salt
> 6 jarred peach halves

Directions:

1. Preheat the oven to 350ºF.
2. In a small pan or dish, combine flour and salt.
3. In a small dish, whisk together the egg and water combination. On a shallow dish, spread cornflake crumbs.
4. To coat the pork chops, dredge them in flour. Dredge each chop in cornflake crumbs after dipping it in the egg mixture.
5. Place the chops over a baking tray that has been lightly coated with non-stick cooking spray. Pour the extra-virgin olive oil over the top.
6. Freeze chops for a minimum of 1 hour after dusting with paprika and salt.
7. Bake pork chops for approximately 40 minutes or unless cooked.
8. Grill strained peach pieces on a grill pan, then serve with a peach piece on top of each pork chop.

NUTRITIONAL VALUES:

Sodium: 262 mg

Potassium: 393 mg

Phosphorus: 202 mg

Protein: 22 g

Carbs: 25 g

Fat: 10 g

GREEN RICE WITH EGGS

SERVINGS: 10

PREPARATION TIME: 10-15 minutes

Ingredients:

> 2 tsp. dark sesame oil
> 2 medium eggs
> 2 egg whites
> 1 tbsp. extra-virgin olive oil
> 1 cup (100 g) bean sprouts
> 1/3 cup (35 g) green onions (chopped)
> 4 cups (750 g) cooked rice (cold)
> 1 cup (155 g) frozen peas (thawed)
> 1/4 tsp. freshly ground black pepper

Directions:

1. Thoroughly mix the sesame oil, eggs, and egg whites in a small bowl and set aside.
2. Heat the extra-virgin olive oil in a large enough non-stick pan, over medium heat.
3. Add the egg mixture and cook until cooked.
4. Add the bean sprouts and green onions and cook for 2 minutes.
5. Then, add the rice and peas and stir-fry until completely cooked.
6. Season with freshly ground black pepper and serve.

NUTRITIONAL VALUES:

Sodium: 37 mg

Potassium: 88 mg

Phosphorus: 66 mg

Protein: 6 g

Carbs: 22 g

Fat: 5 g

SPICY CHICKEN WITH SWEET POTATOES

SERVINGS: 5

PREPARATION TIME: 35-40 minutes

Ingredients:

› 2 tbsp. extra-virgin olive oil
› 1 chopped onion
› 3 minced garlic cloves
› 2 cups (235 g) diced sweet potatoes
› 1 green pepper (chopped)
› 1/2 tsp. chili powder
› 2 tsp. ground cumin
› 1 tsp. dried oregano
› 1 (15 ounces) (425 g) can low-sodium cannel-lini beans, rinsed
› 2 cups (470 ml) low sodium chicken broth or homemade chicken broth
› 1 cup (165 g) frozen corn
› 2 cups (280 g) diced cooked chicken
› 1/3 tsp. fine salt
› ¼ tsp. freshly ground pepper
› Coriander for garnishing

Directions:

1. Heat the oil in a sufficiently large pot over medium heat.

2. Add the garlic, onion, sweet potato, and pepper; stir occasionally and cook for about 5-6 minutes until the vegetables have softened slightly. At this point, add the chili powder, oregano, and cumin and cook, stirring, for about 1 minute. Finally, add the beans and the broth and as soon as it comes to a boil, lower the heat and partially cover, letting it simmer for about 15 minutes.

3. At this point, increase the heat and add the corn, cooking it for 1 minute. Then, add the chicken and cook for another 2 minutes, until hot. Remove from the heat and mix pepper and salt.

4. Serve topped with cilantro and your favorite hot sauce.

NUTRITIONAL VALUES:

Sodium: 383 mg

Potassium: 591 mg

Phosphorus: 294 mg

Protein: 24 g

Carbs: 34 g

Fat: 9 g

MEAT AND ONION PATTIES

SERVINGS: 5

PREPARATION TIME: 1 hour 30 minutes

Ingredients:

> 1 medium potato
> 1 large white onion
> 1/4 cup (30 g) red onion
> 3/4 cup (55 g) lettuce
> 1 pound (450 g) ground beef, lean
> 1 medium egg
> 1/2 tsp. turmeric
> 1/2 tsp. garlic powder
> 1/2 tsp. black pepper
> 1 tsp. Mrs. Dash® herb spice mix
> 4 tbsp. extra-virgin olive oil
> 5 pieces (6 inches) (15 cm) pita bread
> 1/4 cup (6 g) basil leaves

Directions:

1. To minimize potassium, peel and grate the potato, then immerse them in hot water for 2 hours. Using a fresh dish towel, wash, drain, and squeeze out any excess water.

2. Grate the white onion, dice the red onion, and shred the lettuce.

3. Combine ground beef, grated white onion, grated potato, turmeric, egg, powdered garlic, black pepper, and Mrs. Dash spice in a large mixing bowl until well combined.

4. In a medium-sized skillet, heat the oil.

5. Make 5 patties (round, about the size of your hand) and fry until golden on both sides over moderate flame.

6. Dish out each patty with lettuce, red onion, and fresh basil on a pita.

NUTRITIONAL VALUES:

Sodium: 387 mg

Potassium: 467 mg

Phosphorus: 246 mg

Protein: 24 g

Carbs: 38 g

Fat: 20 g

TOFU PASTA WITH CHICKEN AND ASPARAGUS

SERVINGS: 8

PREPARATION TIME: 25 minutes

Ingredients:

- 1 pound (450 g) asparagus spears, flat
- 8 oz. (225 g) chicken breasts, boneless and skinless
- 16 oz. (450 g) raw penne pasta
- 5 tbsp. extra-virgin olive oil
- 1/4 tsp. black pepper
- 1/4 tsp. garlic powder
- 1/2 cup (115 ml) chicken stock (low sodium)
- 1 garlic clove
- 1 ½ tsp. oregano, dry
- 1/4 cup (265 g) extra-firm tofu, shredded

Directions:

1. Snip asparagus, then cut into (1 inch) (2,5 cm) slices on the diagonal. Make cubes out of the chicken.
2. Boil some water in a large saucepan. Cook the pasta according to the package directions, which should take approximately 8-10 minutes. Salt is not needed. Drain the water and put it aside.
3. In a large pan over medium-high heat, heat 3 tablespoons of olive oil. Sprinkle with pepper plus garlic powder before adding the chicken. Cook for 5 minutes, or until the chicken is done completely and browned. Place the chicken on paper towels to absorb any excess liquid.
4. Fill the pan with chicken broth. Add the asparagus, garlic, a dash of garlic powder, dried oregano, and pepper to taste.
5. Cover and steam for 5 minutes, or unless the asparagus is barely tender.
6. Transfer the chicken to the saucepan and reheat it.
7. Mix the chicken mix into the pasta well. Allow 5 minutes to sit.
8. Drizzle the leftover 2 tablespoons of oil over the top, mix and top with extra-firm tofu.

NUTRITIONAL VALUES:

Sodium: 109 mg

Potassium: 242 mg

Phosphorus: 192 mg

Protein: 16 g

Carbs: 48 g

Fat: 11 g

UPPER PENINSULA PASTIES

SERVINGS: 8

PREPARATION TIME: 1 hour 35 minutes

Ingredients:

> 1/4 cup (35 g) carrots
> 1/4 cup (30 g) onion
> 1 pound (450 g) sirloin ground
> 1/4 cup (40 g) frozen corn
> 1/4 cup (40 g) green peas, chilled
> 1 tbsp. Worcestershire sauce (low sodium)
> 1 tsp. freshly ground black pepper
> 1 tsp. thyme, dry
> 1 packet (15 ounces or 2 crusts) (425 g) unbaked pie crust, rolled and chilled
> 1 beaten egg white
> 8 tsp. ketchup

Directions:

1. Preheat the oven to 375ºF. Let the pie crust come to room temperature as directed on the box.
2. Dice the carrots and chop the onions.
3. In a large pan over a moderate flame, cook ground sirloin. Drain the water and put it aside.
4. In a microwave-safe dish, place the carrots. Cook for 2 minutes on medium with 1 tablespoon of water, covered. Microwave for approximately 2 minutes with chilled corn and peas. Drain.
5. To prepare the filling, in a mixing bowl, combine the meat, vegetables, onion, low-sodium Worcestershire sauce, black pepper, and thyme.
6. Flatten pie crusts on a gently floured workspace. Each pie crust should be cut into 4 parts.
7. Half of each piecrust piece should be filled with 1/4 cup of filling. Using a little quantity of soy milk/egg white, lightly wet the pie crust corners.
8. Fold the remaining half of the pie shell over the filling. Crimp the corners with a fork to seal them. Slits should be cut in the tops of the pastries. Using an egg white, coat the top. Put on a large baking sheet that hasn't been oiled.
9. Bake for 15–20 minutes, or until lightly browned on top. On wire racks, cool to room temperature.
10. Serve 1 teaspoon of ketchup on each pasty.

NUTRITIONAL VALUES:

Sodium: 381 mg

Potassium: 213 mg

Phosphorus: 73 mg

Protein: 10 g

Carbs: 29 g

Fat: 21 g

COD FILLETS WITH LEMON AND PIMENTO

SERVINGS: 4

PREPARATION TIME: 20-25 minutes

Ingredients:

> 12 oz. (340 g) cod fillets

> 1 medium lemon

> 1/4 tsp. fine salt

> 1/2 tsp. black pepper

> 1 (4 oz.) (110 g) can pimento peppers, chopped

> 1 tbsp. extra-virgin olive oil

Directions:

1. Preheat the oven to 350ºF.

2. In the prep area, lay down 2 big sheets of heavy-duty aluminum foil.

3. Slice the lemon thinly. Every piece of foil should have half a lemon wedge on it.

4. Set 2 fish fillets or approximately 6 ounces each on foil on top of lemon wedges.

5. Season each fillet with a pinch of salt and pepper.

6. Sprinkle olive oil across each fillet and top with chopped pimentos.

7. To preserve the fish inside, tuck the foil ends together. Bake for 20 minutes on a baking tray. To serve, remove the fillets from the foil.

NUTRITIONAL VALUES: Sodium: 184 mg

Potassium: 438 mg

Phosphorus: 182 mg

Protein: 16 g

Carbs: 5 g

Fat: 4 g

CHAPTER 7:
35 Days Renal-Friendly Meal Plan

This meal plan helps you manage kidney disease by preventing certain minerals from building up in your body, which is very important because your kidneys are not functioning optimally to remove waste products.

Each person is unique and has different nutritional needs. Use the information below as a purely indicative guide. To create a highly personalized meal plan for your condition, it is essential that you are followed up periodically by a dietician.

DAYS	BREAKFAST	LUNCH	SNACK & APPETIZERS	DINNER
1	Red Muesli with Cranberries	Asian Orange Chicken	Strawberry and Blueberry Tofu Smoothie	Green Rice with Eggs
2	Creamy Apple Oats	Couscous with Vegetables	Healthy Baked Falafel	Grilled Salmon Sandwich with Chipotle Mayonnaise
3	Stuffed Biscuits with Bacon and Tofu	Asian Style Turkey and Rice	Delicious Addictive Pretzels	Meat and Onion Patties
4	Creamy Blueberry Oats	Cabbage Borsch	Toasted Pita with Artichoke Relish	Spicy Chicken with Sweet Potatoes
5	Spicy Red and Green Pepper Tofu	Baked Chicken Salad	Stuffed Deviled Eggs	Quinoa with Seared Scallops
6	Creamy Cinnamon Oats	Chicken Vegetable Linguine	Shrimp and Vegetable Rolls	Cod Fillets with Lemon and Pimento
7	Purple Muffins	Barley and Beef Stew	Crispy Brussels Sprouts	Rice with Vegetables and Crispy Tofu
8	The Confetti Omelet	Chicken and Summer Squash Bow-Tie Pasta	Cucumber spread cream	Tuna and Sesame Salad
9	Nourishing Egg Muffins	Chicken Enchiladas	Tilapia Tapas with Adobo Cream	Pork Chops and Peaches
10	Vanilla Pancakes with Berry Jam	Ceviche Caribe	Low Sodium Buffalo Wings	All American Meatloaf
11	Holiday Breakfast French Toast	Chicken Veronique	Grilled Meatballs	Tofu Pasta with Chicken and Asparagus
12	Blueberry Oat Cakes	Challah Holiday Dressing	Chicken Nuggets and Sweet Mustard Sauce	Upper Peninsula Pasties
13	Red Muesli with Cranberries	Couscous with Vegetables	Delicious Addictive Pretzels	Spicy Chicken with Sweet Potatoes

14	Creamy Apple Oats	Asian Style Turkey and Rice	Toasted Pita with Artichoke Relish	Quinoa with Seared Scallops
15	Stuffed Biscuits with Bacon and Tofu	Cabbage Borsch	Stuffed Deviled Eggs	Cod Fillets with Lemon and Pimento
16	Creamy Blueberry Oats	Baked Chicken Salad	Shrimp and Vegetable Rolls	Rice with Vegetables and Crispy Tofu
17	Spicy Red and Green Pepper Tofu	Chicken Vegetable Linguine	Crispy Brussels Sprouts	Tuna and Sesame Salad
18	Creamy Cinnamon Oats	Barley and Beef Stew	Cucumber spread cream	Pork Chops and Peaches
19	Purple Muffins	Chicken and Summer Squash Bow-Tie Pasta	Tilapia Tapas with Adobo Cream	All American Meatloaf
20	The Confetti Omelet	Chicken Enchiladas	Low Sodium Buffalo Wings	Tofu Pasta with Chicken and Asparagus
21	Nourishing Egg Muffins	Ceviche Caribe	Grilled Meatballs	Upper Peninsula Pasties
22	Vanilla Pancakes with Berry Jam	Chicken Veronique	Chicken Nuggets and Sweet Mustard Sauce	Green Rice with Eggs
23	Holiday Breakfast French Toast	Challah Holiday Dressing	Strawberry and Blueberry Tofu Smoothie	Grilled Salmon Sandwich with Chipotle Mayonnaise
24	Blueberry Oat Cakes	Asian Orange Chicken	Healthy Baked Falafel	Meat and Onion Patties
25	Spicy Red and Green Pepper Tofu	Chicken Vegetable Linguine	Crispy Brussels Sprouts	Tuna and Sesame Salad
26	Creamy Cinnamon Oats	Barley and Beef Stew	Cucumber spread cream	Pork Chops and Peaches
27	Purple Muffins	Chicken and Summer Squash Bow-Tie Pasta	Tilapia Tapas with Adobo Cream	All American Meatloaf

Conclusion

The word "kidney disease" (commonly called "renal disease") refers to when the kidneys are damaged and no longer work properly. Kidney disease is curable after it has been diagnosed. However, since it usually goes undetected until serious damage has developed, it's critical to get medical attention if you experience any symptoms.

Chronic kidney disease is a disorder that causes the kidneys to deteriorate over time. Acute renal failure occurs when kidney damage develops rapidly as a consequence of an accident or illness. Even if the injury is minimal, it may cause long-term renal disease. You might need to alter your diet to address your CKD. With the assistance of a professional nutritionist, devise a dietary strategy that comprises foods you like while also maintaining renal health.

The RENAL diet is a straightforward and effective way to lead a healthy lifestyle. It helps in the protection of diseases affecting the kidneys. Don't worry if you're new to the RENAL diet; it's really simple to understand and implement.

What you eat and drink affects your health. Blood pressure may be controlled by maintaining a healthy weight and eating a well-balanced, reduced salt, low-fat diet. If you have diabetes, you can help control your blood pressure by being more careful about what you eat and drink. Managing hypertension and diabetes may help prevent kidney disease from progressing.

A kidney-friendly diet may also help avoid additional damage to the kidneys. To prevent minerals from flowing throughout the body, a kidney-friendly diet limits certain nutrients.

Recipes Index

Made in United States
North Haven, CT
17 June 2023

37848593R00050